From Feather Pen
to Computer Keyboard

From Feather Pen
to Computer Keyboard

✦

Brief Musings on Faith from a 21st
Century Circuit Rider in a Cynical Age

Doug Bower

FROM FEATHER PEN TO COMPUTER KEYBOARD
BRIEF MUSINGS ON FAITH FROM A 21ST CENTURY CIRCUIT RIDER IN A CYNICAL AGE

iUniverse books may be ordered through booksellers or by contacting:

iUniverse
1663 Liberty Drive
Bloomington, IN 47403
www.iuniverse.com
1-800-Authors (1-800-288-4677)

Because of the dynamic nature of the Internet, any web addresses or links contained in this book may have changed since publication and may no longer be valid. The views expressed in this work are solely those of the author and do not necessarily reflect the views of the publisher, and the publisher hereby disclaims any responsibility for them.

Any people depicted in stock imagery provided by Thinkstock are models, and such images are being used for illustrative purposes only. Certain stock imagery © Thinkstock.

ISBN: 978-1-5320-3144-1 (sc)
ISBN: 978-1-5320-3145-8 (e)

Print information available on the last page.

iUniverse rev. date: 08/25/2017

Scripture taken from the New King James Version®. Copyright © 1982 by Thomas Nelson. Used by permission. All rights reserved.

Scripture quotations marked KJV are from the Holy Bible, King James Version (Authorized Version). First published in 1611. Quoted from the KJV Classic Reference Bible, Copyright © 1983 by The Zondervan Corporation.

Contents

Dedication

In the late 60's the Rev. William E. Kircher, while pastor of Oneco United Methodist Church, and his family embraced a shy, withdrawn junior college student. I found a great deal of spiritual support during a pilgrimage filled with questioning while being fundamental in my beliefs. I explored the realms of materials that called the very faith into question. Rev. Kircher made me feel at home. I felt special. I was welcome to explore the faith without a legalism or anxiety that questioning the Christian faith was somehow wrong, not done by people of faith.

Rev. Kircher was really good at adopting people and embracing them. He was also especially good at letting people explore the faith. I feel now that he was good at it because he had confidence the faith could withstand scrutiny. If that was so, he was right. Whether that was the case or not for him, he certainly was secure enough in his faith to feel he didn't need to discourage a testing of scriptures and what the faith stood for.

I lost track of him and his family when I went off to school in Atlanta. This was the mistake of a young person taking it for granted that somehow good relationships continue. I thought I would one day get to sit down with him and thank him for being a part of my pilgrimage. I didn't, to my disappointment.

I am convinced Rev. Kircher played an important role in my faith discoveries. I have long sense been more aggressive about keeping up with such people though still faltering all too often.

Foreword

We are living in spiritually chaotic times. I often find myself as I read scripture, especially the historical books of 1 Kings, 2 Kings, 1 Chronicles, and 2 Chronicles, and feeling like I am seeing the front page of the newspaper. That probably indicates that human behavior hasn't changed very much. It also indicates that when people of faith drift from God, times feel especially difficult.

I would like to think we can talk people into the faith. Fortunately, we cannot. If we could talk people into believing then faith would be in our hands.

A great deal is being said about how to share the faith in our times. There are many books of apologetics, witnessing, and evangelism. I think most, if not all, would agree that we can't talk people into believing. Still, there are many efforts to try.

I have come to believe that while other methods of sharing the faith are important and make sense to some, if not many, it is also important to share one's views of the faith as a person understands it.

In sharing the faith, which has to result from the Holy Spirit working, others may have "ah-ha" experiences. There are those who may come to believe because of faith itself rather than the deliberate effort to convert people.

Lest this sound passive, it is not. It is an active trust that requires interaction with Scripture, word, and tradition. It doesn't occur in a vacuum. When the faith is shared as it is, it touches people's lives. The parable of the sower found in Matthew 13, Mark 4, and Luke 8 illustrate some of the various reactions to the gospel message, or testimonies of faith.

Trust says people will be touched by faith in some way. They may reject it, be hostile towards it, ignore it, or accept it at various levels.

Sharing faith then is important at all levels of understanding, from the complex to the simple.

Acknowledgment

I am not a detail person. The rules of grammar and syntax fall into the detail arena. So to finish this book project I was fortunate in finding help. Sherri E. Dickens of GhostSecPro, LLC is the person who put the finishing touches on the project. She didn't do any editing save for correcting my grammatical mistakes and finding typing and spelling errors. Her effort was greatly appreciated.

Our Human Situation

Just over 30 years ago, I wrote the following unpublished statement. "We are living in the most confusing, frustrating and depressing age that has ever been seen in the history of the human race. It is confusing, because the very values of an 'older generation' had been challenged by a 'younger generation.'" Both generations were scarred. The younger generation made its challenge because it had been bombed and bombarded with so many different ideals and concepts that it did not know who or what to believe. The problems that emerged were issues society had to face: What to do with all the pluralism, what to do with all the different ideals that are real in this society because of our exposure to the world, what to do with the changes in morality, and what to do with conflict among people and nations.

The confusion caused frustration as an older generation helplessly watched its young struggle for ideals and in so doing resisted the attempts of their elders to show how much they cared through the sharing of their ideals. It was a very frustrating time for the nation and the world. The searchers were frustrated because they could not really find an answer or a set of ideals. Those who were satisfied with the ideals they inherited were frustrated because their values are being challenged. They felt pressed to conform.

The confusion and frustration lead to depression because in the search for meaning, all of us had to come to face the reality that we could destroy ourselves by war or pollution. We had to come face to face with the reality that we had been cheating our brother and sisters because of various reasons. We had come to realize our crime rate is escalating and problems are escalating.

Yet our confusion, our frustration, our depression, has occurred at a time in history when people have accomplished great works through knowledge. We have virtually eliminated small pox, plague, yellow fever, tetanus, and polio as medical problems in this country. We put men on the moon and

1

provided more social services for the needs of our people. There are more human rights available to all people than ever before and there is more food available than ever before. We can go farther and faster than any generation could before us and communicate better with almost every point on the globe.

In a new century, there is nothing new to say. The 2010 mid-term elections were claimed to be among the most contentious, and certainly the most expensive in our country's history.

We can destroy the world with just a push of the appropriate "buttons." Terrorism has replaced or supplemented nuclear anxiety. Instead of fearing the communists, we fear terrorists. Instead of small pox, plague and the like killing our people, cancer, stroke and heart disease are killing our people. The automobiles we use and the planes we fly are eating away at our resources. The great factories we have built to provide jobs for the economy are upsetting the environment. The economy struggles under the weight of jobs shifting to cheaper work forces and less regulations in other countries. The government spends money it doesn't have and misspends money that is supposed to be used to help people. The social security fund set up for the elderly is grossly inadequate and threats of collapse linger.

Harvey Cox said in the July 1977 issue of Psychology Today there was a "searching for truth, brotherhood and authority." In 2009, Cox wrote "the dance of science has increased the sense of awe we feel that the inmates scale of the universe or the complexity of the human eye. People turn to religion war for support in their efforts to live in this world and make it better, and less to prepare for the next" (p. 3.). Considering there are close to 7 billion people in the world, Cox's statement is rather presumptuous. However, it seems consistent with his 1977 statement and probably does capture something of today's human condition.

Why were we and are we having the problems in spite of our goodness and if I may say, greatness. Well, the psychologists like Freud Fromm said it is because of our self-destruction. We learned or developed this self-destruction because we are all mistreated to some extent during childhood. We are programmed wrong. We have too much guilt. We are not dealing with anger properly. We don't assert ourselves properly, etc, etc.

Yet, it has been interesting to me to note that though modern thinking believes that all the problems of the world can be eliminated and solved through science, medicine, psychology, sociology and technology, the problems seem to be getting bigger instead of smaller. Uncounted books, articles, and media materials have predicted doom, even as uncounted materials praise incredible advances.

It is also interesting to me to note that there has been an explanation for our human situation which has been in existence for a least a couple of thousands of years and parts longer than that. This explanation is found in the Bible. Oh, the terminology is different, but it says the same thing we are saying today.

It says that the cause of man's ills is Sin and because of Sin man is facing the dilemmas of life.

But what is Sin?

Billy Graham, in his book "How to be Born Again", said that Sin is "missing the target" saying further that "one of the translations of the term sin in the New Testament means 'a missing of the target!' Sin is a failure to live up to God's standards (p. 69). Later, he wrote "we are all sinners by choice" (p. 70).

Yet somehow this seems inadequate for it states that we keep ourselves missing the mark. As Mr. Graham said, "Christ faced . . . temptations in the wilderness. He over-came all of them and there by showed us that it is possible to resist the temptations of Satan . . ." (p. 67). His statement forgets we are not ourselves Christs and that Christ was God and without Sin. We are with Sin. We were born into this mess of sin. We might choose sinful behaviors, but we don't choose to be sinners. We became sinners as soon as we entered life. We do not choose this. It is imposed upon us. The consequences are dramatic and often traumatic.

So then, what does Wesley say about Sin? Wesley looks at Sin as that which is inherited by man through the Fall of Adam. However, for Wesley there were two sides of Sin: the deliberate and the unintentional Sin.

Deliberate sin is that which a person consciously and intentionally commits. It is outward sin and is sin which is the outward transgression of the law.

Unintentional Sin is inward sin and is that which is at the very core of the human being. It is the hopeless corruption of the person which effects the physical being, the mental being, and the spiritual being. Wesley described this Sin saying, "But how am I fallen from the glory of God! I feel that I am sold under sin.' I know, that I too deserve nothing but wrath, being full of all abominations: And having no good thing in me, to atone for them, or to remove the wrath of God. All my works, my righteousness, my prayers, need an atonement for themselves. So that my mouth is stopped. I have nothing to plead. God is holy, I am unholy. God is a consuming fire: I am altogether a sinner, meet to be consumed" (p. 113).

Wesley, I believe came very close to understanding the nature of Sin. I disagree with his feeling concerning outward, deliberate Sin. Wesley, as I have said, indicates this can be controlled by the individual. However, we see outward Sin in all Christians. Therefore, I would like to suggest that outward Sin is a symptom of our corruption.

I decided to turn next to John Calvin to see what he says concerning Sin and was amazed that I came to a conclusion about Sin which was and is similar to Calvin's. Calvin would have agreed with Wesley that Sin has outward manifestations, but Calvin's look at it says "original sin, therefore, seems to be a hereditary depravity and corruption of our nature, diffused into all parts of the soul, which makes us liable to God's wrath, then also brings forth in us those works which Scripture calls 'works of the flesh' (Gal. 5:19), and that is properly what Paul often calls Sin. The works which come forth from it - such as adulteries, fornications, thefts, hatreds, murders, carousing, - he accordingly calls 'fruits of sin' (Gal. 5:19-21)" (p. 251). Calvin also says that "we are so vitiated and perverted in every part of our nature that by this great corruption we stand justly condemned and convicted before God, to whom nothing is acceptable but righteousness, innocence, and purity" (p. 251), to which I add we have none. Also Calvin says "this perversity never ceases in us, but continually bears new fruits – the works of the flesh that we have already described" (p. 251).

However, in considering Sin, we must not forget that the male and female were created in the Image of God. It needs to be seen that with the Fall, the creation that was pronounced good by God. It did not stop being good, but also became bad. This means that within us all there is something of the diving image "Imago Dei." Faded as it may be, blinded as we may be to it, we are able to create. We are able to respond to human needs. We are able to love ourselves and others. We are able to see a dim light through our blindness. This enables us to grasp that God exists.

Because of our goodness, we have responded to needs of people and provided care, and love and comfort. Because of our goodness, we have made efforts to make communication with each other more meaningful and more accurate. Because of our goodness, we attempted to make the world a better place to live in even though it is debatable whether or not we have succeeded.

Now, because of the two sides of our human situation, we need to maintain a balance between our awareness of our sinfulness and our goodness.

We must never become so caught up in our awareness of Sin and corruption and our depravity that we lose sight of the fact we are creatures of God. We are important enough for God to have sent His Son into the world to redeem us. We also must never think we are so good we should be entitled to God's love and thus forget we are sinners, lost, rebellious and deserving only of eternal punishment for our sins.

This balance is difficult to maintain. But, by turning to God and realizing that He loved us enough to send His Son to redeem us, we begin to allow the Holy Spirit to work in us to maintain the balance concerning our human situation. Through the Holy Spirit we become aware of our sinfulness and our goodness and turn to God for our salvation and redemption.

References

Czalvin, J. (1960). *Calvin: Institutes of the Christian religion, Volume 1* (John T. McNeill, Ed., Ford Lewis Battles, Trans.). Philadelphia: The Westminster Press.

Cox, H. (1977). Eastern Cults and Western Culture: Why young Americans are buying oriental religions. *Psychology Today* (July): 36-42.

Cox, H. (2009). *The future of faith.* New York, New York: HarperOne.

Wesley, J. (1997). The Ages digital library collected works: The works of John Wesley, Volume I, Journals, Oct. 14, 1735 - Nov. 29, 1745. Albany, OR: *Books For The Ages*, AGES Software, Version 1.0, p. 113.

Our Need For A Savior

I want to discuss with you thoughts on our need for a savior. In the last chapter, I made comments on our human situation. In relationship to that theme, I can state the following. In the beginning, God created the heavens and the earth. On the sixth day of God's creation, He created male and female in the image of God. He pronounced this aspect of creation as the others, "good."

Then came the Fall, and the creation that was good now also became bad. Keep in mind that in the Biblical account, Satan was lurking about. Evil existed before creation. It tends to be overlooked in this story. Perhaps evil and sin became so synonymous that this was/is easy to do. Sin is introduced with the Fall. Death, destruction, error, murder, fornication and the like became a part of the creation. The human being became corrupt, deprived, rebellious, egotistic, narcissistic, and sinful and began to consciously and unconsciously defy and transgress the will of the Lord God. In short, Sin became part of the world.

In recent years, having been influenced by a contemporary humanistic view that human beings are basically good, I have paid more attention to the positive aspects of being a creature of God. Again, the Genesis account says that human beings were created in the image of God and were pronounced "good." Surely, that hasn't disappeared. The Calvinists assert that human beings are totally corrupt. That gives a great deal of power to sin to have completely ruined God's creative act.

I now believe the original nature of human beings has been distorted making it impossible for us to function as God created. Thus, death, destruction, and sin persist.

I have also come to believe that being made in the image of God placed great creative and resourceful powers in the hands the Adam and Eve.

Fortunately, they partook of the fruit of the tree of knowledge of good and evil and were ousted from the Garden of Eden before they could partake of the tree of life. Lord, knows what a mess things would be if they had been able to get to the tree of life. In their original state, when they fell, they took the whole of creation with them. Thus death and destruction is not limited to human beings. It infects every aspect of creation.

On November 16, 2010, a story hit the news about scientists photographing the birth of a black hole. The black hole resulted from the demise of supernova SN 1979c in the early 80s. It is evidence of the destructive realities in the universe and thus in creation itself. We actually don't have to look to outer space to see this destruction. A story on the same day reported the collapse of a building in India that killed a number of people.

One of the questions of skeptics in our time asks, "How can a good God allow bad things to happen?" To me the answer rests in part with the power of the destructive acts that came with the Fall. It also rests in the following answer: God didn't allow bad things to happen. He engaged the realities that have, do, and will unfold with grace and ultimately through the life, death, and resurrection of Jesus Christ.

It is precisely at this point and for this reason that we need to have a savior. So I want to take this space to be more specific in regards to our need for a savior. I am going to place these specifics in four general categories: theological, psychological, sociological, and physical.

First, the theological needs for a savior. I believe the major theological problem for us and the world is our almost blindness to God. We simply cannot seem to grasp the light and thus we go around following almost anything which looks like it has promise. Let me illustrate.

About a year and a half ago, a young man handed me a book about Ekankar. He proceeded to testify to the wonderfulness of this great and marvelous religion if you will. According to Ekankar.com, "Eckankar means "Co-worker with God." It offers ways to explore your own unique and natural relationship with the Divine." Ekankar provides peace and tranquility the young man said. I turned down the offer to read the book, but my curiosity as to what Ekankar was drove me toward reading the book. I also listened to the young man accuse me of being closed minded and decided to read the book to find out what the basic idea of Ekankar was.

As I read, it didn't take long to find out the meaning of Ekankar. It is soul traveling and advocates that one, at will, can remove the soul from the body and do as one pleases and go where one pleases. I suppose a significant appeal of this concept is that at death one removes the soul from the body or rather the soul leaves the body.

I had one question for this person. I asked him, "Supposing that soul traveling is a reality which can be accomplished, what about those of us who cannot grasp the ideas of Ekankar, are we to be left out of the peace and tranquility that Ekankar is supposed to offer?"

I am convinced the Christian faith, while espousing peace, joy, and love, etc., does not rest upon those experiences in relationship to salvation. I don't have to grasp the ideas of Christianity to be saved. The act of salvation comes from what God did for me and everyone through the life, death, and resurrection of Jesus Christ. Not everyone though wants this salvation and thus rejects it. "This is the judgment, that the Light has come into the world, and men loved the darkness rather than the Light, for their deeds were evil. For everyone who does evil hates the Light, and does not come to the Light for fear that his deeds will be exposed" John 3:19-20 (NASB). Jesus says this far more strongly than I would. I see it as saying there are people not wanting to have anything to do with God.

Another illustration applies to this issue.

I was approached by another young man and he was very ecstatic. He proudly announced he had led his girlfriend back through three previous lives. Needless to say, I was very skeptical but listened to his story. He described to me two of the past lives of this girl saying that she saw herself in a bulky dress with petty coats and described the shoes she was wearing. He also said she was an Indian and described the death of this Indian as death by a knife wound in the back.

The young man claimed everyone was reincarnated and could get in touch with their past lives by a super self-consciousness. The technique for this was discussed with me. I am hardly in a position to describe the technique. Further, I haven't seen another person who made such a claim or demonstrated a similar capability. I figure that while my world is pretty small in the scheme of things, I do have enough broadness to my world to have at least seen this again. I have not.

I also keep wondering, is reincarnation salvation? It sounds like a trap to repeat a variation of the same old patterns though with different twists to them.

I had several questions for this young man for he wanted to know how Christianity could reject this ideal and be so closed minded about it. I said it denies the sovereignty of God and also denies the uniqueness of individuals.

I left him with one question. If, as being said today, there are as many people living today as there has been in all of history before this generation, how do we all have multiple reincarnations? I suppose an answer would be this could be the first time for them. Or maybe they were reincarnated from a different creature that became human. These sound entirely too absurd.

I offer these stories as part of the multi-religion picture, we have Buddhists, Muslims, Hindus, Jews, Hari Krishnas, Bahai and on and on the list goes. Even in Christianity we have more denominations than we can adequately keep track of.

What does this point to? One of the things it points to is our blindness to God. Because we are blind to God, we need God to save us for we cannot save ourselves. We cannot even agree on how salvation comes about.

Other theological problems which indicate we need a savior are, and I will not illustrate these here, rebelliousness to God, rejection of God, elevating ourselves to the level of a God, which is impossible for we are only able to fool ourselves into believing that we are God. There are many things to be thought of here, but time does not permit.

Next, there are psychological indications for a need of a savior. This area in our lives is loaded with examples. Just walk into any bookstore, there is tons of literature. One of our problems, which indicate our need for a savior, is our search for self-understanding. New titles keep emerging addressing this personal issue.

Many years ago, I read a book called "I'm OK, You're OK." It is a book dealing with transactional analysis which is a popularized interpretation of the work of Freud concerning the three levels or aspects of the human mind, id, super ego, and ego. There may be some disagreement of the experts on my asserting this. However, I remain satisfied of my simple description. Transactional analysis calls these child, parent, and adult.

Basically transactional analysis says our problems in life are caused by the child, or parent in us controlling our lives. It says that for life to be meaningful, to be satisfying, the human mind must be controlled by the adult in us. For it is the inner adult which provides a balance of our child and parent. When the adult is in control, we communicate better with others, especially those who have their adult in control. When the adult is in control, our anxieties and fears are reduced and life becomes less traumatic. The theory state that to obtain this, all one has to do is to turn over our behavior to our adult by an act of will. It may not be all that far from what Carl Rogers called the "fully functioning person." This person is secure, creative, balanced, and resourceful.

Though there were many who swore by transactional analysis, I am not convinced the world is a better place in which to live because of it. An atheist friend of mine, who was very familiar with the person-centered approach of Carl Rogers, said before she died, "The world is going to hell." She, as a humanist, saw deterioration in human behavior in spite of so many different theories of psychology and psychotherapy. I still see an awful lot of confused, disillusioned and apathetic people in this world who are not successful in making life better for themselves. The fact there is still so much literature on the market today concerning how to make life more satisfying points to this. Some of the titles include: "The Erroneous Zones," "Games People Play," "How to be Loved," "How to Live with Another Person," "Getting Together," "The Angry Book," "Don't Say Yes, When You Want to Say No," "On Personal Power," "The Anger Trap" and many, many, more show the expanse of the literature. The list seems endless. It only shows how hungry we, as a people, are for a satisfying and meaningful life. It also shows how desperately we need God to make life meaningful for us, because despite the arguments that we can make life meaningful for ourselves, I haven't yet seen the person who has. Assuming that such a person or person does exist, there are so many who struggle showing how frail human beings are psychologically.

There are several other psychological problems which inform us we need a savior and again, because of time, I will only mention them here. We cannot get along with each other frequently, we get confused and are apathetic toward a troubled world and others and there are other problems. Books4selfhelp.com lists the following mental health concerns addressed by the popular literature of our time: Abusive Relationships, Addictions, Anger Management, Anxiety and Panic Disorder, Bipolar Disorder, Body Image Distortions, Depression, Eating Disorders, Narcissistic Personality Disorder, Obsessive-Compulsive Disorder, Post-Traumatic Stress Disorder, Recovery from Child Abuse, Social Anxiety, and Suicide.

How weak we are with all these possible problems.

There are also sociological reasons for believing we need a savior. The major sociological problem which indicates this is war. Nations cannot agree and thus go to war. We only have to look at the history of this country to see this. There was the Revolutionary War, the French and Indian War, the Civil War, the Spanish-American War, World War I, World War II, the Korean Conflict, Vietnam, Desert Storm, Iraq, and Afghanistan. War, War, War, War, War. If ever there was a club that was, and is, hitting us over the head to tell us we need a savior, it is War. Need I say more? I think not.

Other sociological problems are almost anticlimactic here, but will be mentioned. Crime, hunger, poverty, racism, bigotry, child abuse, spouse abuse, and divorce are just a few of the sociological problems that demonstrate to us we need a savior. Thousands of years of history, and interactions among human beings and there is not an indication that human behavior has improved.

Finally, there are physical problems which demonstrate to us we need a savior. I would like to discuss two of them. Disease and illness will be considered first. Illness is important here because it strikes everybody whether it is a cold or heart disease; all of us become ill in some way.

My first venture into the medical profession occurred when I was still in high school. I started working in the medical profession as a respiratory therapist (before licensure) and eventually became a Registered Nurse. I have seen a lot of sickness and disease. I have watched people suffer from appendicitis, arthritis, colitis, inflammation of the gall bladder, intestinal obstruction, broken bones, head injuries, eye infections, and many, many other problems. I am convinced that we, as people, are in an impossible situation and illness demonstrates how helpless we are in this world. Oh we can prevent and cure a lot of diseases, but if one thing doesn't get to us other things will. All of us will perish.

To show you how susceptible we are to illness, I would like to use myself as an example. I am a healthy specimen, more or less. I know I am a fairly healthy person. However, I have had all the basic childhood diseases, chickenpox, measles, and mumps. In 1969, I discovered that I had a blockage of the ureter (tube) which drains my left kidney, and it had caused my left kidney to expand to about twice its normal size. I underwent surgery to correct the problem and it was found that a measly little ole blood vessel was wrapped around the ureter, constricting it. Following surgery for several years I would develop kidney stones though I no longer get these. In 1972, I got pleuritis and pneumonia. Since then, I have had a variety problems needing medical assistance from kidney stones to nasal blockage. However, in 2006, I discovered I had prostate cancer. To date, I am approaching 5 years without a reoccurrence of the disease. Suddenly, I look upon my health record and don't feel so good about it. I see my physical frailty.

What I want you to see is that I am helpless before the problems of disease and illness. I am not helpless in being able to deal with illness, but I am helpless in that even if I didn't have any physical problems, there would come a day in which I did.

Now, I must address the second physical problem which demonstrates we need a savior. It is death. And it is death which shows more than anything else how desperately everyone needs a savior, because everyone has to face death. No one has been able to defy death. We may be able to postpone it, but it will come.

I remember the first time I participated in cardiopulmonary resuscitation. It was being done to try to save a man who was about 50 years old. Things seemed to be going well with the procedures and measures taken. I was handling the chest compressions. I do not remember a heart monitor and would not have been able to understand it at the time anyway, but after several minutes of effort there was a sudden change in the tone of the man. He went totally limp. We continued efforts a while longer, but were unsuccessful at savings the man's life. To this day, I am convinced that the moment I felt the changes in body tone was the moment we lost that man. And I remember when we finally gave up, I looked down at my hands and said to myself, "I felt the moment that he died." I knew when it was over.

Here is one last physical illustration. Almost 40 years ago my grandfather died. It was sudden and surprising and left me and the rest of the family stunned and confused. It came at a time in which I was wondering about the integrity of the scriptures. I remember one night a number of years later painfully facing the possibility that one day my life would also end. There would no longer be any consciousness and awareness and I would no longer be able to appreciate the world and its people and creatures. It was agonizing.

I began searching the scriptures for evidence which would clearly state that Jesus Christ was raised from the dead. Since the Gospels at this time were questionable to me, I turned to Paul and found the answer for which I was looking. But before I show you what I found, I want you to see that in my grandfather's death and my reaction to that death, there is more evidence for a need for a savior.

Now here is what I found. "Moreover, brethren, I declare unto you the gospel which I preached unto you, which also ye have received, and wherein ye stand; By which also ye are saved, if ye keep in memory what I preached unto you, unless ye have believed in vain. For I delivered unto you first of all that which I also received, how that Christ died for our sins according to the scriptures; And that he was buried, and that he rose again the third day according to the scriptures: And that he was seen of Cephas, then of the twelve: After that, he was seen of above five hundred brethren at once; of whom the greater part remain unto this present, but some are fallen asleep.

After that, he was seen of James; then of all the apostles. And last of all he was seen of me also, as of one born out of due time" 1 Corinthians 15:1-8 (KJV).

I found relief for my angst in these verses. However, death looms before us. There is nothing in our own ability and merit that we can do about it. Death is the ultimate reflection of our need for salvation.

It is right here that I want to proclaim to you that the savior we need is seen in Jesus Christ. In Jesus Christ, God has saved us from our sins, our inadequacies and our corruption that we might have eternal life. God has defeated Sin and Death for us.

The Hope of That to Come

One of the problems I have had with Christianity has been what to do with error, prejudice, pain, suffering and death among Christians. The atheistic question, "if there is a God, how can He let these things happen?" is challenging. However, the raising of the question points one on a track to find an answer.

In my own early Christian pilgrimage, I heard all too many times a theology from pulpits that emphasized, if one only accepts Christ as Lord and Savior, then life will not have the pain and suffering which is seen in non-believers. In fact, as I attempted to network during setting up my counseling practice, I had ministers indicate that all anyone needs is Jesus to fix mental problems. Indeed there is a lot of support for this argument floating around. Stories of people whose lives were changed after being confronted by Christ are numerous and readily available from the right sources for hearing and reading. They are often used to attempt to bolster the case that people with problems simply need to turn their lives over to Jesus and things will be OK. Yet there are discrepancies with each of them.

There is the story of Peter the fisherman. A very meaningful story, for here a brash, perhaps young man, was approached by the Christ and called into His service. Peter went and followed Christ. He witnessed the greatest miracles ever seen, people healed, the blind cured, the lame walk, fever removed, five thousand fed, storms calmed and walking on water by Jesus and Peter himself. As a result of his experiences with Christ, Peter became the very rock of faith that Christ said he would.

Yet, this same Peter is the one who denied Christ three times. He is the same Peter who refused to witness to the gentiles. He is the same Peter who argued violently with Paul. And he is the same Peter who died just like another human being.

Then there is Paul, a man who persecuted the Church and condoned the killing of people of the Way. After a direct confrontation with Christ on the road to Damascus, he became the greatest preacher and evangelist for Christ ever seen in the world. He went all over the existing world about the Mediterranean Sea preaching Christ. Further, his letters have been one of the great witnesses to Christ found in Scripture.

Yet, this same Paul is the one who fought belligerently over Mark and refused to have him accompany him on his journeys. This same Paul, turned out to be so very egotistical and self-centered in his writings, just look at the number of times he said "I." He is the same Paul, who, like Peter, died just as any other person would and does.

I would like to pull now to a more contemporary scene. The late Oral Roberts was as viable a witness to the Christian testimony as anyone. Here was a man who had TB and was on his death bed but was healed of the disease. Because of that healing, he too became a healer in Christ.

Yet, this man built a prayer tower that cost a fortune, while starvation, disease, pollution, and a variety of atrocious problems exist in the world.

Billy Graham is another fine evangelist who has been instrumental in proclaiming the word of God to the world. His ministry has led thousands to accept the saving work of Jesus Christ.

Yet his organization has amassed millions of dollars while millions of people starve.

Now let me come down to a more normal or average level and also look at pain and suffering in the process.

One of my dearest friends in high school and with whom I worshiped frequently got married to a fine young man. They had a baby boy. However the boy was born a mongoloid.

You can bet your life they prayed for a normal child, but did not get one.

While I worshiped at Oglethorpe United Methodist Church (now closed), a young woman with two children started worshiping there. She was very faithful to the Church and came nearly every Sunday. However, the youngest girl had an incurable disease. You can bet your life that many prayers have been offered to God for the child's healing, yet there is no healing.

Both of these examples have been subject to "if only you let Christ control your life, then everything will be taken care of" or "if only you have enough faith you'll get the answer to your prayers."

How many of us have seen a person, maybe a relative, in need of deliverance from a problem only to see that person wallow in pain, suffering and tribulation even though we prayed for that person or the person prayed for himself or herself?

In another direction, how many times have we seen someone converted to Christ who was an alcoholic delivered from alcoholism only to jeopardize life with cigarettes?

Years ago, we picked up the newspaper and saw that Catholics and Protestants in Ireland were killing each other: Christians against Christians. Today, perhaps like never before it is religion against religion.

How many times have we refused, to help someone because they did not have the same status in life economically as we do or because their skin or culture was different from ours.

In light of these examples, are we to reject the notion that when Christ comes into our lives we are changed? Absolutely not! Lives are changed through Christ. Rebirth does take place. However, our rebirth is not complete. Our change is not finished.

It is in rebirth that we see what to do with prejudice, error, pain, suffering, tribulation, and death. We know these arise because Sin is in the world. Therefore, since these still exist in us, the people of God, it is logical to conclude that Sin still exists in us. Even though we are taught we can purge Sin from ourselves by faith through Jesus Christ, in harsh reality, Sin by the Grace of God is allowed to exist in us.

To say that God allows sin to exist isn't a very good statement. I have come to believe that God is not allowing Sin to exist in us. Rather, his disallowance for Sin occurs through the life, death, and resurrection of Jesus Christ. Sinners expect God to act differently towards Sin than he has. We either expect Him to condone it, or remove it. Instead, God addresses the problem of Sin through the cross and resurrection.

It is promised in scripture that we will be made whole when we turn to Christ. Should we reject this promise? Again, by no means!

We will indeed be made whole. Sin will be eliminated from us. And with it, error, prejudice, pain suffering, tribulation, and death will also be eliminated.

For, now, we will have error, we will have prejudice, we will have pain, suffering, tribulation, and death. And for the time being will have Sin as a part of our lives.

However, again, God has confronted his displeasure with Sin through Jesus Christ. Through Christ, God offers forgiveness, not rationalization to continue in Sin.

However, there is coming a day when the Lord God Almighty is going to destroy Sin and restore this creation to that which he had intended. There will be peace in the world because we will be able to get along with each other. We will no longer experience pain, suffering, tribulation and death. "And I heard a great voice out of heaven saying, Behold, the tabernacle of God is with men, and he will dwell with them, and they shall be his people, and God himself shall be with them, and be their God. And God shall wipe away all tears from their eyes; and there shall be no more death, neither sorrow, nor crying, neither shall there be any more pain: for the former things are passed away" Revelation 21:3-4 (KJV).

We will no longer be subject to error and prejudice. The world will be under God's control, free from Sin and free from the temptations of Satan. It will be full of willing, loving, caring people. We will love God with all our hearts, minds, and souls and love our neighbors as ourselves. We will be perfect as our heavenly father is perfect. We will obey all the laws of God because they will want to obey them. We will do so because we will know that life is meaningful, satisfying. It will be best to live that way.

There will be harmony with nature as is it meant to be. The lamb and the wolf (Isaiah 11:6) will lay down beside each other (with no harm coming to the weaker of the two). The human being will not misuse the environment and destroy the ecology for there will be no greed or ignorance.

So in the face of Sin, in the face of error and prejudice, in the face of pain and suffering and tribulation and death, there is hope. This is our hope in addition to our hope for redemption in Christ and the comfort we receive through the Holy Spirit, that God Almighty, maker of heaven and earth, deliverer of the children of Israel time after time, sender of our Redeemer Jesus Christ, will remove the purge of Sin from the land, He will clearly reveal Himself to all. "For it is written, As I live, saith the Lord, every knee shall bow to me, and every tongue shall confess to God" Romans 14:11 (KJV).

It is here that we find another source of strength for our predicament in life. The history of Israel is one aspect of our hope. The resurrection of Christ is another aspect of our hope. The presence of the Holy Spirit is still another aspect. Yet another is the hope of that to come.

With these, we can find courage to face the problems of life, for we have hope that God will ultimately restore creation to its original state through the resurrected Christ who will return from his ascension into heaven to claim His people and His world.

Until that time, we have the comfort of the Holy Spirit who helps us realize that God created this earth, delivered the children of Israel, sent His Son into the world to redeem it, and will return and set up His kingdom in a way there will be no doubt about what happened.

This is our claim. This is our hope. We believe that we can only believe this because we are informed by the Holy Spirit.

PRAISE THE LORD FOR OUR DELIVERANCE!

The Importance of Worship

In July 1977, I had the privilege of preparing my first sermon. So many years later, I don't remember why I decided to address the importance of worship in that first sermon project. I simply did.

My views on worship haven't changed a whole lot on that topic. As I reviewed the material, I found I still hold similar positions.

The preparation of the sermon was the most difficult of the few sermons I had prepared up until that time. In fact it was harder to prepare than my first sermon, because it was for keeps. I was no longer experimenting on a congregation made up of seminary peers. The first sermon allowed me to practice for a real congregation within a pastoral context. I was joining with a congregation to which I had become its pastor. Even though it was a student appointment, it was not an experiment for school. It was a work for our Lord, with and for, His people.

Therefore, there was real pressure to function and to act. In the past, I had let sermons develop. In this first official occasion, I began to push and to try to make a sermon. The sermon topic was easy enough, but somehow the research was not registering. I became anxious, almost panicky.

Then I put some principles to work. I had been reading some material on Christian life and faith by Oral Roberts. I no longer remember which resource I had been reading. I suspect it had material on seed faith. In the material, Oral Roberts pointed out that God is the source of life, power and inspiration. I took this to heart and decided to let the sermon develop under the idea that God is the source of His message and inspiration, and not Doug Bower. I am an informed person, but it is the Spirit who gives life or perhaps inspiration to what comes out of my head and my mouth. This life comes not from the words I say or do. My words convey life, but God will use the words to His glory and give life. There is a flavor of "And the Word was made flesh, and dwelt among us, (and we beheld his glory, the glory as of the only begotten of the Father,) full of grace and truth" John 1:14 (KJV).

This is not an issue of delusions of grandeur. Rather, it is a claim that God works powerfully and persistently in people. Not everyone tends to this work. In faith, the work is realized and actualized. One becomes aware that God is speaking through regular ole language. In this case it is English. The preacher declares the substance of the nonverbal revelation, if you will, through language. This declaration is not limited to the preacher. The preacher is simply ordained by the Church, singling him or her out to proclaim the word as the Word is made manifest in faith.

Though I had struggled to develop the material, I decided to stick to the original topic.

So "the Importance of Worship" became one of my first sermons.

The rationale for sticking with the topic hasn't changed in those 30 + years. There had been, and there continues to be, much criticism of worship by Church goers and non-Church goers. Christians and non-Christians have said worship is dull, boring, irrelevant, impractical and uninteresting.

In response to this, worship has been changed, added to, turned upside down, inside out and every-which way, in an effort to make it more exciting, more interesting, more attractive, and more relevant to the people. However, this has failed even though there are examples of exciting worship around the country. These exciting experiences tend to be limited to collections of very talented individuals. Thus, I say it has failed because people with less talent can hardly pull this off in "normal" Churches. Even prerecorded back-up music remains prerecorded back up music offered by musicians who otherwise wouldn't be given the time of day by more talented worship leaders.

All the changes have not helped change our realization of the importance of worship. Instead of going to Church, people still go to the lake. Instead of getting up on Sunday, people stay up late on Saturday and sleep late on Sunday, saying the reason we avoid worship is because of the problems it has. Knowing the problems doesn't seem to have helped most of us.

I assert that grasping the importance of worship is what takes the boredom, disinterest, and apathy out of worship, not the changes or the talent. Good talent can distract people from their doldrums. However, it takes revelation to take people out of their complacency (if that is a good word here).

I am proposing the significance of worship comes from another source. That source is God. It is here where we must examine the importance of worship.

What is worship? Think about it a second. What is worship? It is going to be a hard question to answer.

While I would hope to answer that question with ease, I find myself wondering if I will indeed accomplish that. Paul Waitman Hoon (1971) said, "The meaning of Christian worship can only be known by worshiping men" (p. 24). This may then be more of an experiential definition or description than an intellectual one.

I have thought about this question concerning worship many times over the years. However, when I tried thinking about how to share my thoughts, I found it difficult to put together the words. It was helpful to reflect on a discussion I had with a couple of nurses at Northside Hospital in Atlanta years ago. During the discussion, these two persons cut down worship and Church and advocated that one could worship individually and did not have to go to Church in order to worship.

I claimed worship was not worship unless two or more people joined together to celebrate in the presence of God. Worship to me could not be individualistic because it requires not only interaction between a person and God but also interaction between or among persons.

I have since changed this position. I realized David and Daniel of Old Testament times worshiped God alone without others around. Worship, I conclude now, can take place on an individualistic basis. It is not an individualism which deliberately chooses to reject congregational worship because of perceived inadequacies of worship. Worship by individuals supplements congregational worship with private worship. It may also occur out of necessity when a person does not have access to a congregation.

I still have not answered the question. What is worship? And if you haven't heard anything else, please hear this, worship is what happens when we focus on God and Jesus Christ by adoration, illumination, confession, and dedication. In short, worship is responding to God. Again (Hoon, 1971), "In the transaction between God and man through Jesus Christ in Christian worship, the Church is constituted, called into being, knows and confesses her true being, and reveals her being" (p. 34). Hoon later says, "Christian worship is God's revelation of himself in Jesus Christ and man's response; that it is the dialogue between man and God through the Word; that it is Christian's priestly action kindling the priestly action of the faithful . . . that is encounter of Christ in his Real Presence with the human soul" (p. 77).

This leads us to another question. Why do we worship? Or why do we respond to God? This question is just as hard to answer as the first question.

In the past, I have not thought much about the question and maybe have taken it too much for granted. Therefore, I have struggled here for an answer.

I had to do a lot of reading to find that for which I was looking and spent many hours trying to search for an answer which would be satisfactory to me so I could share it. Basically, this is what I found out and I want you to grasp this.

We worship God because God has done something for us. He has interacted with us through the Holy Spirit to help us understand His saving act in Jesus Christ. We have responded to God, are responding to God and will respond to God because of what God has done, is doing, and will do in Jesus Christ. It is about as Brett Scott Provance (2009) said, "reverence rendered to God" (p. 130).

We join together in worship because this act of God in Christ is so powerful that even in our sinfulness, our lack of excitement, our lack of interest, we feel the need or desire to praise His Holy name. The interaction is so strong we want to be with others in responding to God's loving, saving work for His creation and the people of that creation.

When we realize our need for a savior and let God interact with us, we must worship in some way. Perhaps the following verses apply: "That which was from the beginning, which we have heard, which we have seen with our eyes, which we have looked upon, and our hands have handled, of the Word of life; (For the life was manifested, and we have seen it, and bear witness, and shew unto you that eternal life, which was with the Father, and was manifested unto us;) That which we have seen and heard declare we unto you, that ye also may have fellowship with us: and truly our fellowship is with the Father, and with his Son Jesus Christ. And these things write we unto you, that your joy may be full" 1 John 1:1-4 (KJV).

If worship is in part about fellowship, then certainly these verses describe something of the compelling nature within us to worship. Worship may lack excitement or it may be thrilling depending upon how much we have come to understand our need for a savior. Also, how much we have come to understand and accept that God has indeed provided a Redeemer for us in Christ has an impact. "Rejoice in the Lord alway: and again I say, Rejoice" Philippians 4:4 (KJV).

This in turn results from how much faith God has given us and how much faith we accept from God. Some of us will have much faith and others of us will struggle to believe. However, the more we ask of God, the more we accept from God and the more we allow God to work in our lives, the more we realize God is working in our lives. This, even if we may not see or believe He is working. "Jesus saith unto him, Thomas, because thou hast seen me, thou hast believed: blessed are they that have not seen, and yet have believed" John 20:29 (KJV). As people of faith grasp this, worship becomes more exciting. It becomes more attractive as it is a powerful responding to God. We want to participate in worship.

With an understanding of God's act which results from the witness of the Holy Spirit in our lives and with our accepting of God's work so we can respond, we can no longer dismiss worship as unimportant. We can no longer look upon worship as boring and the like. We can realize that the excitement of worship does not come from what we do in response to God. Nor does our attitude determine the importance of worship. Rather, the excitement of worship rests in our realization of what God has done in Jesus Christ. Excitement comes in direct proportion to our realization of God's act in Jesus Christ. Our realization rests in how much we allow God to witness to us concerning life in Jesus Christ.

Our challenge is to accept God's witnessing Spirit. We can let it help us respond meaningfully, enthusiastically, and firmly to God's saving work in Jesus Christ. When we do this, the people will come. Churches and congregations will grow. People will want to join with us in responding to God's love. We will want them to be with us in this experience because it is too good to hide from a world that faces worry, anxiety, depression, pain, suffering, crime, war, and death. In worship we celebrate a belief that God has acted, is acting, and will continue to act to deliver us from the mess called reality.

References

Hoon, P. W. (1971). The integrity of worship: Ecumenical and pastoral studies in liturgical theology. Nashville, TN: Abingdon Press.

Provance, B. S. (2009). Pocket dictionary of liturgy & worship. Downers Grove, IL: InterVarsity Press.

Essentials of Worship

This chapter is hardly exhaustive regarding the essentials of worship. I am making assumptions that the elements contained here are necessary to the worship experience. Others may believe other elements or worship are essential that aren't mentioned here.

Fellowship

In Psalms we see one of several similar threads. "O come, let us worship and bow down: let us kneel before the LORD our maker" Psalm 95:6 (KJV).

Why Fellowship?

It is unstated. The Bible doesn't appear to openly mandate the connection between fellowship and worship. The above verse doesn't even mention the word fellowship. I found no overt connection in my search. There are no Bible verses containing the words "fellowship" and "worship."

It is implied. "Let us Worship." Fellowship is in the word "us." We get together to worship. It is often an event of a believing community.

For years, I thought the key to worship was an issue of finding ways to make the structure of worship more exciting. I also thought more exciting sermons, or lively music would be important keys to better worship. There are exceptional preachers and musicians that indeed add excitement to worship experiences. There are outstanding musicians who can light up a congregation. However, the exceptional talent is the exception for most Churches.

I am finding myself believing that fellowship, real fellowship, is where the excitement and enthusiasm are. An important key then to worship would then not be talent. It would be the interaction that occurs in fellowship.

Unfortunately, fellowship has been suppressed and squelched by creating formal worship structures. Formal worship is important. However, can we have our cake and eat it too? That is, can we have formal worship and fellowship together?

Fellowship is automatic. John wrote fellowship goes beyond worship experiences while being in worship. "That which we have seen and heard declare we unto you, that ye also may have fellowship with us: and truly our fellowship is with the Father, and with his Son Jesus Christ. And these things write we unto you, that your joy may be full" 1 John 1:3-4 (KJV). It occurs to me, that proclamation, and thus certainly real hearing of proclamation, establishes automatic fellowship.

This fellowship is two-fold. However, the word "we" in fellowship may not involve others. Fellowship initially occurs in relationship to God. This in turn, puts us into a relationship with other believers. Fellowship results from our interaction with God and comes automatically with seeing, hearing, and proclaiming. This brings us together under God.

The second aspect is about joy. Fellowship is about joy. "These things we write, so that our joy may be made complete." This is evident when people celebrate because they are connected with God and with one another. I am now convinced it is fellowship over all the other neat experiences of faith that adds substance to faith and thus to worship. The joy comes when we are able to be open to the experience of fellowship. When we are not in fellowship, we are often left feeling disconnected from God and certainly from each other.

Another part of the element of fellowship is related to not being aware of our fellowship. Fellowship may occur in relationship to God though we may not feel psychologically or socially connected to God or to one another. It is illustrated nicely by the following expression of faith: "Why standest thou afar off, O LORD? why hidest thou thyself in times of trouble?"

Psalm 10:1 (KJV). It is doubtful that God disappears. This verse is an appeal to God out of a sense of disconnection, which in reality doesn't exist. God hasn't given up fellowship with us under these circumstances. We simply have lost a sense of awareness of God's presence.

Further, there is a bunch of shy people in the world. There is a bunch of angry people in the world. It is not unusual for people to feel like they are not engaged in fellowship even in a crowded room. Is God absent because we fail to grasp His presence? I doubt it.

Can we push on our sense of fellowship? That is, can we develop awareness that faith is the result of fellowship with God whether we consciously feel connected or not? Can we assume that we are having fellowship with God, even if we feel disconnected socially to one another?

Faith shouldn't be limited to whether we actually feel connected to God or not. For instance, another Psalmist wrote, "How long wilt thou forget me, O LORD? for ever? how long wilt thou hide thy face from me?" Psalm 13:1 (KJV). This too is a statement of faith while reflecting something of the mental state of the believer. We are connected through faith though at times feeling alienated.

The fellowship we have with God is automatic, not dependent on how we feel or what we experience. We are in a relationship with God regardless of our experience. A way to have that fellowship and relationship with God and community is through worship.

Fellowship is also deliberate. We can choose to have this fellowship. We decide to worship. Can we push on it further? Can we decide that we will be satisfied with worship?

There may be some conditions here which may include the social fellowship we have and have decided to make a part of our worship experience. The conditions may include whether we deliberately enjoy our worship and fellowship, or be satisfied or not.

One source (Unknown, 2010) said, "You are responsible for your thinking. Change your thinking and life will get better. But, what thoughts do you change? Your troublesome thoughts about a situation can easily be found in your self-talk. Self-talk is that inner running dialogue you have with yourself. It is what you tell yourself about life's situations."

Personally, I think this change is deeper than what we think. Faith is a dramatic change which has been known to impact life changes. Faith also can have an impact on our perceptions of fellowship and fellowship can have an impact on how much we value worship.

If what I am saying is true, then fellowship is persistent or universal. Of all the experiences we can have in worship, I am convinced that fellowship is the most durable, baring violation of our relationships.

If miracles are important, they don't occur persistently in our lives. If prayer is important, we don't always engage in prayer. If sermons are important, they are all too often dull and uninteresting.

Fellowship is the only experience in worship and faith is constant and which is both the result of our interaction with God, and with others.

I used to go to lunch frequently on Mondays with men who made up the Athens Full Gospel Businessmen's Fellowship. I didn't go to speak in tongues or see miracles, or hear power testimonies. I went because of the fellowship.

The same is true for worship. I don't go to preach or pray. I go, because I value the fellowship. Fellowship remains my primary reason for worship and association.

It is my observation the Church is alive that has powerful fellowship opportunities.

Prayer

Invocation

We begin our worship with prayer. We call on God to touch us and be with us. Of course, God already is doing that. However, this is an occasion of our deliberately joining together in face to focus upon God as He touches us.

Henry Fields (2010) offered this prayer. "Father, you have given us every good thing we need to make life meaningful for everyone. This morning we especially thank you for the love of Jesus Christ, who came to set things right and still abides carrying out his purpose in our generation and time. Hear our prayers, especially the one Jesus taught his followers and which together we pray in your presence" (p. 216).

Does God need to hear these things? No. Prayer is not for God, it is for us. Prayer gets us ready for God, not God ready for us.

Pastoral Prayer

The pastoral prayer is about our concerns and celebrations. John Thompson (2007) offered this prayer:

"Dear God, how we need a bridge across the chasm separating us from the rest of the human race—a bridge to span the space between the darkness of loneliness and the light of belonging. How we need to leave the caves of our self-seeking and selfishness, and walk forth into the light of the vision that your love for all persons and peoples inspires. But when we see man's inhumanity to man, it is difficult sometimes for us to hold on to that vision.

For leaders in the community of nations pursuing ways of peace, we pray wisdom and courage that foundations of justice may be laid, that the hungry may receive bread, the naked clothes, the refugees and homeless home and housing. Open our eyes to see the new thing you are doing in our day and rejoice. We pray shalom, well-being, wholeness for all those suffering brokenness of mind, body, and spirit among us. We pray for them an increase of faith that they may be open to receive the healing, the wholeness, the life that you will for them. When life-threatening illnesses threaten any of us, grant to us that peace that the world cannot give and that the world cannot take away. Through him who is our peace" (p. 146).

In a few brief moments a wide spectrum of interests is presented in the above prayer. Again, the prayer is not for God. God knows about the material presented. The prayer is for those who worship and are focusing on God.

<u>Offertory Prayer</u>

Assuming Lee McClone (2010) prepared this offertory prayer, let us consider it. "Lord, you know the greatness of many small gifts — and all our gifts are small compared to the grandeur of your gifts to us. Increase the measure of our love, so that our offerings may worthily magnify your name. Amen."

We prepare our hearts, minds, and souls for offering. This is an occasion for us to prepare to reach out the world around us. Here we prepare to give in response to God's gifts.

<u>Sermon</u>

I prepare to engage every sermon with prayer. I don't know of any formal rationale for this, save it has been done traditionally and there is always room for another prayer. "It will strike every man who thinks about it, that there should be some preparation of the heart in coming to the worship of God and to the hearing of the Gospel" (Spurgeon, 1885, p. 2). We can also consider Paul's exhortation to "Pray without ceasing" 1 Thessalonians 5:17 (KJV) as a rationale for the prayer before a sermon. I have to think along with Spurgeon in terms of the sermon prayer being about preparing our minds to hear God's word.

After all we have to cut through the words of the preacher and trust that God's voice is heard over and above what the preacher proclaims. After all preachers are sinners. God has to be behind, above, and within the preaching.

The end of the sermon also contains prayer. I think of this in terms of approaching God about our grasping something of what God has for us.

Purposes of Prayer (Not Just Worship)

Prayer is, in part, about our distress and concerns. "How long shall I take counsel in my soul, having sorrow in my heart daily? how long shall mine enemy be exalted over me?"

Psalm 13:2 (KJV). In this prayer is a statement of faith. This is a Psalm attributed to David. It comes out of his faith in the face of personal difficulty. There is no statement of the specifics. The enemy is not defined. The enemy for any given person could be a disease, a conflict with another, discouragement, an obstacle, a struggle with the faith, anything.

Prayer gives us a means within worship and outside of worship to engage God with our struggles. Sometimes those struggles come to an immediate end with a miracle. However, I am far more impressed with prayer that engages ongoing struggles and reflects faith in the absence of a miracle. I wonder then if prayer is not a miracle.

Prayer is also about celebration and thanksgiving. This may be the most difficult aspect of worship and prayer. When prayer concerns are presented, the celebrations are the hardest to come by. No matter what group, joy experiences are not as plentiful.

The book of Psalms is loaded with such expressions of joy. Here are some examples. "O clap your hands, all ye people; shout unto God with the voice of triumph" Psalm 47:1 (KJV). "Great is the LORD, and greatly to be praised in the city of our God, in the mountain of his holiness" Psalm 48:1 (KJV). "Make a joyful noise unto God, all ye lands" Psalm 66:1 (KJV).

This celebration and thanksgiving doesn't have to a jumping up and down experience. It might be. It can simply be "Thank you, Lord, for saving my soul, Thank you, Lord, for making me whole; Thank you, Lord, for giving to me, Thy great salvation so rich and free" (Sykes, 1948 & 1968).

Music and Song

In 2 Chronicles we see this awesome experience. "It came even to pass, as the trumpeters and singers were as one, to make one sound to be heard in praising and thanking the LORD; and when they lifted up their voice with the trumpets and cymbals and instruments of musick, and praised the LORD, saying, For he is good; for his mercy endureth for ever: that then the house was filled with a cloud, even the house of the LORD" 2 Chronicles 5:13 (KJV).

Apart from the cloud filling the temple, music has a special character. Music is the spice of worship. It gives expression to worship. If fellowship is the heart of worship, music, next to hugs and handshakes, gives life to worship.

It is assumed that large Churches draw people because of their programs. I submit their success is greatly related to their music programs.

The problem is the better their programs become, the harder it is to be anything more than an observer, even if you are pretty good in music. Competition sets in and perceptions of those having the most pleasing skills are held up as stars for God and thus of the local Church. A handful of talented individuals dominate the worship experience.

Still the music can be awesome to experiences in the midst of great talent. The Mormon Tabernacle Choir comes to mind in thinking about great music.

Some Principles To Consider

Music and song is about a joyful noise. "Sing forth the honor of his name: make his praise glorious" Psalms 66:2 (KJV). It doesn't say, make an excellent noise unto God.

When I was growing up in Oneco, Florida, between Bradenton and Sarasota, I sang in the Oneco Methodist choir. We might have had 12 - 20 people singing. We were not particularly impressive.

However, the choir took a great deal of pride in singing. No one in the choir would have dared try out for a major music ensemble. No one would have qualified.

In another Church in which I served briefly as an interim pastor, there was a man who sang in the choir. You could hear him above everyone else. Even as the congregation sang, he could be heard above everyone else. He was noticeable not because of his volume, but because he sang out of key. He was a monotone. The sound was awful. However, he loved to sing and make a joyful noise. No one thought of asking him not to sing. He set the standard for joy.

We sing because of God's awesome works. This is the cause of the joy. In these works God has touched our lives and we celebrate God's willingness to deal with us.

Music and song are about "a New Song." The basis of a new song is this: "I will sing a new song unto thee, O God: upon a psaltery and an instrument of ten strings will I sing praises unto thee" Psalm 144:9 (KJV).

Here are some of the ingredients of the new song. They are not present in every song that is sung. However, they will be found in every legitimate or official hymnal. There is recognition that God is the creator. "So God created man in his own image, in the image of God created he him; male and female created he them. And God blessed them, and God said unto them, Be fruitful, and multiply, and replenish the earth, and subdue it: and have dominion over the fish of the sea, and over the fowl of the air, and over every living thing that moveth upon the earth" Genesis 1:27-28 (KJV).

Being awesomely and wonderfully made, we can be amazed not only at how incredible the human being is, but also all the other creatures around us. I am a creationist myself, not because the Bible says that we are created by God, but because of the complexity of what makes us human and other creatures what they are. For instance the DNA apparatus is so complex that it has only been recently that it has been mapped with the help of computers. Yet it is so diverse that various arrangements make it possible for roaches, jellyfish, bees, pine trees, and humans to exist all using the same atoms and molecules.

Ever walked along a path and run into one strand of a spider's web? That spiders can do that amazes me. That it happened by accident or coincidence as nature created itself escapes me. There is too much intelligence involved for spiders to have figured out how to do that. How did they become capable of creating spider webs all by themselves? Faith, points to God as creator giving creatures such capabilities.

We sing a new song of redemption, and salvation. To have this new song, we recognize the brokenness of all creation and certainly the human condition.

Sin is persistent. It ruins lives, disrupts daily routines, is behind greed, selfishness, immorality, and alienation from God.

God has overcome it, even as sin continues. It is often asked how God can allow evil and atrocity to occur. God doesn't allow it. He responds to it with an offer of forgiveness and redemption. God addresses evil by His standards not ours.

Thus, the question is the wrong question. What did God do about sin?

He sent his son. "For God so loved the world that he gave his only begotten Son, that whosoever believeth in him should not perish, but have everlasting life. For God sent not his Son into the world to condemn the world; but that the world through him might be saved" John 3:16-17 (KJV). A variation of this is at the heart of the new song we sing.

God could have responded to the death of his son with fire and brimstone. He did so with Sodom and Gomorrah for far less. This was Jesus who was put on the cross. Yet, God forgave sin for the whole world. All someone has to do is accept the gift. All too many don't and then seek something different from God.

The new song is about celebration.

The world is full of hate, violence, chaos, greed, and selfishness. It needs a new song. We get to sing it during worship. "O come, let us sing unto the LORD: let us make a joyful noise to the rock of our salvation" Psalm 95:1 (KJV). Celebration takes us to a higher place. It helps us deal with the realities of hardship. It helps make life more peaceful and pleasant.

Word

Undergirding everything that our faith stands for is the Word. "In the beginning was the Word, and the Word was with God, and the Word was God" John 1:1 (KJV). So there is no worship without it.

A Very Brief Theology

There is a great controversy in our time. It surrounds this snapshot statement: biblical words equal infallibility and inerrancy. It is stated that the Bible is inerrant.

Verbal battles have been and are waged. Attitudes dashed or offended with claims that the Bible is inaccurate.

Personally, I see little of the battle in history. However, I didn't look for the issue during my required studies of Church and Biblical histories during my pilgrimage. There are those who did. "The Bible did not claim inerrancy for itself, but Fundamentalists devised or discovered elaborate philosophical defenses of the idea. How it came to be picked up and then reinforced in the twenties and early thirties is an important element in the story of schism and reshaping in the Protestant majority between the wars" (Marty, pp. 205-206). It seems to me to be a contemporary issue.

The Bible has been in the hands of sinners for 2000 years and that it has survived is a miracle. I think its survival says a great deal about the Holy Spirit being behind its creation, its impact, and its endurance.

Translations have scarred it and thus distorted it. Which translation is infallible or inerrant? There certainly are significant discrepancies among the various English translations. There are even greater discrepancies among the translations of the different languages. Lest someone hold that it is the Greek or Hebrew texts that are inerrant, which Greek and Hebrew version does one choose. There are a host of different versions that differ greatly in the Greek manuscripts (Metzger, 1971).

I resolved the controversy for myself. Mistakes or errors, if they exist, don't bother me. I have followed several claims concerning mistakes over the years, but often leave them flabbergasted at the lack of support. There seems to a great deal of misinterpretation of texts leading to claims of errors. The Greek text differences are interesting, but don't shake my sense of the significance of Scripture.

The Bible is sufficient for pointing to God. In my own pilgrimage I wrestled with the legitimacy of Scripture. I left that struggle having a sense that the writers of Scripture absolutely positively believed in the God about whom they wrote. Their words pointed to the wondrous deeds of the Lord and also to the words of the Lord. "And afterward Moses and Aaron went in, and told Pharaoh, Thus saith the LORD God of Israel, Let my people go, that they may hold a feast unto me in the wilderness" Exodus 5:1 (KJV).

Also, belief is possible without it as the early Church didn't even have the documents we have now. When Jesus called his disciples, there was no New Testament. At the Pentecost event, there was no book of Acts. Romans was probably written before Luke and certainly before John. Members of the early Church compelled to write, wrote those documents now called the New Testament.

Next, John said, the Word is God and became flesh (John 1:14). It didn't say the Bible is God. The Bible points to the inerrant Word and it is Jesus Christ and God. It has long struck me that for the Bible to be infallible and inerrant, it would have to be God. It is not. It is a collection of works showing us the way to God. It does not have to be inerrant, if it were it would itself be divine.

Further, if I can believe in the greatness of George Washington, or Mozart, with all the disagreement and error in their biographies, certainly I can trust the writers of Scriptures concerning their observations. Surely, the Bible has as much integrity as any great work.

The Word in Worship

The Holy Spirit is the heart of the Word in Worship. There is no worship without God and thus without the Word as Holy Spirit.

Since Jesus is no longer physically present, the Word is actualized by the Holy Spirit. We encounter God through the Holy Spirit. "Wherefore I give you to understand, that no man speaking by the Spirit of God calleth Jesus accursed: and that no man can say that Jesus is the Lord, but by the Holy Ghost" 1 Corinthians 12:3 (KJV). Thus, the Holy Spirit is significant to the worship experience.

In this encounter, we are not puppets in this, doing the bidding of God.

If I meet someone, I may decide to speak about that person or I may not. If I am impacted powerfully by that person, negatively or positively, I am at least inclined to think about the person or tell others.

So it is with worship. If we feel touched by God, we are inclined to worship God. We may, however, decide to speak about God or not. Hopefully we will prefer to speak about God through our participation in worship.

Testimony

The Full Gospel Businessmen's Fellowship was built upon testimony. Men would give examples of how they were healed or had occasions of speaking in tongues.

The radical nature of their testimonies brought criticism and skepticism. However, for many years, until recently, the organization thrived.

I don't remember seeing formal testimonies in worship services during my life time. There were some informal experiences in which I saw them. Most had a flavor of what God did for me and what God can do for you.

The Fellowship of Christian Athletes among others is open to testimony. The organization in part is growing because of the testimonies of athletes at a variety of meetings. The testimony is an important part of what FCA does.

In a community sing-a-long in Bishop, GA, we introduced the concept of an interview style of witnessing. At first we simply had a songfest. Then we added an interview. It had the flavor of a mini-roast of the interviewee and was great fun while offering witness to Jesus Christ in the lives of the participants.

Scripture

I am very biased about this area. Scripture is the foundation of the verbal aspect of faith. It gives us the words that go with grasping what we encounter God in the Holy Spirit.

A concept of Prevenient Grace asserts that God engages preparing us, or calling us to accept God's grace and act of salvation. Without words, this experience remains just outside of our grasp. Scripture gives us the words.

In the Old Testament (2 Kings 23), Josiah, after learning about the existence of the Book of Scriptures had the whole book read to the people of Israel. "And the king went up into the house of the LORD, and all the men of Judah and all the inhabitants of Jerusalem with him, and the priests, and the prophets, and all the people, both small and great: and he read in their ears all the words of the book of the covenant which was found in the house of the LORD" 2 Kings 23:2 (KJV).

While we can get away with worship by not having individual testimony, we cannot get away from Scripture. "All scripture is given by inspiration of God, and is profitable for doctrine, for reproof, for correction, for instruction in righteousness: That the man of God may be perfect, throughly furnished unto all good works" 2 Timothy 3:16-17 (KJV).

We don't have to read the whole work during our worship as Josiah did, but Scripture gives the basis for worship and the Word which is behind and within the worship experiences.

<u>Sermon</u>

At one time, a 2 or 3 hour sermon wasn't unusual.

There are a few occasions where an hour sermon is still preached by exceptionally talented and blessed preachers.

In the Black tradition, long sermons are still preached with high energy.

For the most part, those days are gone. Our tolerance, perhaps altered by television and radio with commercials has made it difficult to focus very long.

My own bias again is that the sermon's integrity is rooted in scripture. Length is not the issue. There is no sermon without scripture. The sermon coupled with scripture is the ultimate testimony, if you will. "For whosoever shall call upon the name of the Lord shall be saved. How then shall they call on him in whom they have not believed? and how shall they believe in him of whom they have not heard? and how shall they hear without a preacher? And how shall they preach, except they be sent? as it is written, How beautiful are the feet of them that preach the gospel of peace, and bring glad tidings of good things!" Romans 10:13-15 (KJV)

The word undergirds our worship experience. Without it, what we do is just another human activity. With it, we engage God and substance is given to the worship experience

References

Fields, H. (2010). Invocation. In Lee McGlone (Ed.). The Minister's Manual: 2010 Edition. San Francisco, CA: Jossey-Bass.

Marty, M. (1991). Modern American Religion, Volume 2: The Noise of Conflict, 1919-1941. Chicago, IL: The University of Chicago Press.

McGlone, L. (2010). Offertory prayer. In Lee McGlone (Ed.). The Minister's Manual: 2010 Edition. San Francisco, CA: Jossey-Bass, p. 216.

Metzger, B. M. (1971). A textual commentary on the Greek New Testament. New York: United Bible Societies.

Spurgeon, C. H. (1885). Before sermon, at sermon and after sermon, no. 1847: A sermon delivered on Lord's-day morning, June 28, 1885, at the Metropolitan Tabernacle, Newington. www.spurgeongems.org/vols31-33/chs1847.pdf

Sykes, S. & Sykes B. (1940, 1968). Thank you, Lord. Grand Rapids, MI: Singspiration Music, Zondervan. http://my.homewithgod.com/heavenlymidis2/tyl.html

Thompson, J. (2007). Prayer. In James Cox, & Lee McGlone (Eds.). The Minister's Manual: 2007. San Francisco, CA: Jossey-Bass, p. 146

Making Contact with Christ:
Reflections and Recollection of a First Offering of Communion

It has long since been the first time I had the privilege of administering the sacrament of Holy Communion. I felt it was and is still important to share my views on the Lord's Supper. I wonder, if then and now, we as Christians hear about its significance. In fact, I cannot remember the last time I heard a sermon concerning such an important aspect of Church life. Of course, as a preacher, I don't get to hear sermons regularly in a Church. However, I don't have a recollection of deliberately looking for sermons on the topic either. I also don't recall really finding them incidentally to exploring other sermons as I made efforts to not get stuck in preaching ruts. I cannot even recall a Church School lesson which covered the subject. My exposure to the significance of the Lord's Supper has been in the worship, preaching courses I had taken at seminary, and the reading which I have done.

So, I think I'll take this opportunity to offer a little information or material on this sacrament. I also want to offer some thoughts that, I hope, will help in grasping the significance of Communion.

I would imagine that during the first Lord's Supper the disciples said something to themselves to the effect of "What are you talking about Jesus?" I mean, they must have been awfully confused.

First, Christ tells them that one of them is going to betray him.

Next, they get hit with "Take eat, take drink, do this in remembrance of me, for I will not take of food or drink until the kingdom comes."

Jesus also hits them with who is the greatest, servant or master?

And they must have asked, "What is going on here?" It must have been terribly puzzling.

39

Then came the ultimate in confusion. Jesus was indeed betrayed and the betrayal takes place at the hands of Judas. Jesus is taken, tried, and crucified until dead. It was a brutal, atrocious scenario.

The event of Jesus' capture was enough to strike fear and terror into the hearts of the disciples. FLEE! FLEE! RUN FOR YOUR LIVES! WHERE CAN I HIDE?

Jesus, the Messiah dies on the cross.

There was absolute heartache and grief. OH NO! OH NO! WHAT WILL WE DO? WHAT IS GOING TO HAPPEN TO US? WILL THEY CRUCIFY US ALSO? HELP US! HELP US! I am not convinced that most of Jesus' immediate followers were not much more than teenagers, at best being in their early 20's, if that.

However low and behold, an empty tomb was reported by Mary. It was seen by Peter also, but still there was doubt.

The disciples gather together in Galilee. Amazingly the resurrected Jesus arrives. Doubting Thomas who was not present said this was not for real. The dead do not rise from the dead. Fortunately, Thomas is confronted with the real wounds and the real Jesus, a Jesus who could not have lived through the conditions he encountered. Here He was, raised from the dead. Thomas realized this and believed.

From the time Jesus ascended into heaven, until their own deaths, the disciples understand they are to share the Lord's Supper. It becomes an encounter of the experience of Christ's death. It further becomes one of the ways of remembering the crucified Jesus who has risen from the dead.

Of course, the disciples do die and the significance of the Lord's Supper is placed in the hands of their followers. These people did not partake of the first Lord's Supper, so obviously some of its significance in knowing Christ is lost. They simply weren't there. They never were directly caught up in the events and experiences directly related to the Passion of Jesus. At some point, the people who were there no longer were alive to share their experiences directly. No longer are there people alive who knew whether or not the death and resurrection really took place. A trust in the validity of reports and testimonies sets in. There had to be people who took the words passed on seriously. A new generation must now rely on the witness of the Holy Spirit as captured in a tradition which we know now has survived for about 2000 years.

At the same time, something very important has to confirm the testimonies of the tradition. It is the ability of encountering God in a way that transcends the physical arena. It is with the witness of the Holy Spirit that the meaning of the Jesus event survives in the Lord's Supper.

Later generations at first took the story of Jesus to be true but then began to interpret the meaning of the Lord's Supper in relation to Jesus is various ways. The Catholic Church, being the only Church, produced the idea of Transubstantiation developed by a person named Paschasius Radbertus and later adopted as essential to real faith. Basically, what transubstantiation says is that in the elements Christ's real flesh is found. It would be the same as eating a real person. While I reject that notion, it certainly captures how significant and powerful the Lord's Supper was viewed.

Luther later asserted that this is not quite right. He thus developed the idea of Consubstantiation. Basically this says that although the real presence was indeed manifested in the bread and wine. It could only be grasped when the believer partook of the elements.

Then Ulrich Zwingli came along and said this is rubbish. The words "this is my body, and blood" are only a metaphor and not to be taken in the literal since at all.

Here we find most of us modern "believers." We agree with Zwingli. This is only a symbolic event. However, in interpreting it this way we have lost appreciation for the Lord's Supper. It is now a mechanical event. Commercially made breads are marketed and taste like cardboard. Wine has become grape juice with the remaining amounts thrown away and easily discarded.

So, is there realism to the Lord's Supper? Yes!

First, it is significant because it is an event which reminds us of a past event, namely Christ's death. It is a death that only has significance because of His resurrection. Without resurrection, it is just another death. There have been billions of deaths.

In relationship to resurrection, it was a death which was God's sacrifice to redeem the people of His creation.

The resurrection was significant to show that Jesus was and is who He said He was and is.

Second, encountering the elements of bread and cup is a means of grace. I prefer to think of it is a means of grace because the encounter is with Jesus via the Holy Spirit. If there is a real presence, it is not a presence that we see. It is a presence we experience. Partaking of the elements is another way of having this powerful experience in God. I also wonder if the desire to even take Communion is in part about the Holy Spirit calling us to engage Jesus.

The final significance of the Lord's Supper comes in the realization that Christ's death, resurrection, and present work in our lives through the Holy Spirit is not all there is. For, as Christ pointed out, He will not eat or drink again until the kingdom comes. Here we see that one day God Himself is going to return and establish peace on earth. Sin will be eliminated and with this elimination death also will be eliminated. There will be life everlasting and we will see God, walk with God and talk with God in a way that there will no longer be any doubt in our hearts that Jesus Christ is Lord.

The Holy Catholic Church

One Sunday after church, a member was talking with me about the meaning of the Holy Catholic Church and the Communion of Saints. He said he had never heard a sermon pertaining to the Holy Catholic Church or the Communion of Saints. I told him that he had just given me two sermon topics with which to work. I didn't feel I could carry on an adequate conversation with him concerning these subjects at the time. So we didn't discuss it very long at all.

I decided to put together a sermon concerning the Holy Catholic Church. Now, I didn't know how inspiring the sermon would be. It seemed more appropriate as a topic for Sunday School. I had hopes that some inspiration could come through the thoughts I presented. I had no recollection if I was successful in regards to inspiring anyone. I do remember the person who made the inquiry never returned to Church again. Apparently, he had a history of dropping in once in a great while and then disappearing.

The topic of the Holy Catholic Church turned out to be and remains extremely complicated and extremely controversial. So, what I am about to say is not the final word on this subject. If I were to choose to write about the subject on another occasion, I might make different observations.

However, I now endeavor to come to some sort of an understanding or at least an explanation of what the Holy Catholic Church is.

Many, perhaps, have heard the story of the man who got to heaven and was given a tour by Saint Peter. They come upon one group of people. They were having a joyful time and the man asked who they were. St. Peter replied, "Why these are the Baptists."

As the man and St. Peter go farther, they come across another group who are also having a good time. Again the man inquired about them and was told they were the Catholics.

They approached group after group. Each time he finds out who they are, the Episcopalians, the Presbyterians, and on and on. Finally, they came to a huge door and St. Peter quietly opened it. Inside is the last group of people and they are having a good time just like everyone else. However, the man asked who these people were and why they were behind the door separating them from the others. St. Peter replied, "These are the Methodists. They think they are the only ones here."

This could be told on any denomination. It is not to pick on us Methodists, for the denominations are interchangeable here and all were guilty of thinking their denomination is the only one which has the correct interpretation of Scripture and the tradition. That has changed in recent years. I heard Charles Stanley, a Baptist affirm other denominations recently. We, as Methodists, can note that our attitude of John Wesley who said something to the effect, it pleased God to give to Methodists the one true way. His battles with Calvinists are well known to Methodist explorers. Clearly, he thought they were wrong and he had it right.

As I grew up a Methodist, I was taught the one true way was that other denominations teach truth concerning the Gospel. The followers within these denominations were saved. In fact, I can remember at a Church league softball game, a couple of the ball players were talking about Methodists and Catholics and ended their conversation by saying, "It doesn't make any difference. We are going to the same place anyway."

I seek now to explore the significance of the Holy Catholic Church. I am going to look at the phrase backwards. First, let's look at what the Church is. Second, what is the meaning of Catholic. And lastly, we will deal with the significance of Holy.

First, let us look at what the Church is. It needs to be understood that the Church is not an institution. Though the institution represents a collection of the representatives or officials of the Church, we cannot limit thinking of the Church as an institution or structural entity. The Church is not an organization even though there are organizational aspects within the Church.

The Church is the people of God. That is to say all those who belong to God make up the Church. They are the people who are under the realm and reign of God. These people of God allow the Holy Spirit to have an influence in their lives so they may be able to at least hope in God's saving work. Those who are people of God try to be obedient and to love God. They are people of God because God has taken them into his work of redemption which he extends to all people in his creation. "For we are labourers together with God:

ye are God's husbandry, ye are God's building" 1 Corinthians 3:9 (KJV). Paul indicates some separation here that I don't accept. I tend to think the Church as a whole is the "we" of this passage. Those who aren't in it are the "you."

It is well known that not all people accept God's work of redemption. There are those who reject it with violent acts, and there are those who simply reject God's act of redemption because they don't like the message.

The Church is next, the body of believers. In order to become a person in the Church, one has to believe in the saving work of Jesus Christ which God has provided for all the people of his creation. Those who believe have responded to what God has done in Jesus Christ. They have accepted his act of redemption. So in this way, those who respond to Christ are now the body of believers. The body of believers is the sum total of all those who have acknowledged Christ as savior and Lord.

The Church lastly, is the body of Christ. Now this aspect is much harder to describe, but let me try. The human body has many parts and functions, but central to it is the head. The body carries out the functions which many times originate in the head. The nervous impulses which guide the functions begin as signals from the brain.

There are a host of other aspects of the body which make a human body possible: heart, stomach, liver, bones, skin, muscles, etc. These all work together to make a human body what it is.

So it is with the Church, the body of Christ. It is the Church which carries out the functions of the head of the Church, Jesus Christ. It is through the people of God, the body of believers that Christ continues to work in the world. Not that this is the only way God works in the world, for it is not, but it is through the Church that the Gospel is communicated to the world.

Yes, God works in the world apart from the body of believers by preparing the hearts of nonbelievers, but until the witness of believers reaches their ears the non-believer has no idea about what is happening in the heart.

Second, what is the meaning of the word Catholic. Hans Kung (1967) in his book entitled simply "The Church" wrote, "The word 'catholic' — the adverb is kaq' o{lou, or the later adjective, kaqolikov-, rendered in Latin by the loan-word "*catholicus*" or "*universalis*" – means:

referring to or directed towards the whole, general" (p. 296). He also goes on to say that the word kaq j o{lou is never used in association with the Church in the New Testament. Kung said that Ignatius of Antioch applied the word catholic to the Church in New Testament times sometime before

110 AD saying "Wherever, the Bishop is there the people should be, just as, where Jesus Christ, there is the Catholic Church" (p. 207).

During the third century AD the word catholic had its accent shifted: that Church and those Christians "are called 'Catholic' who are united in the whole Church, and not, like the heretics, separated from it. The word 'Catholic' in fact takes on the sense of 'orthodox': instead of the reality of catholicity there developed the claim to catholicity" (p. 298). This, in essence, means that as the Church reacted against heretical and misguiding movements, it over reacted by insisting the organizational Church was the Church. And this theme has remained to this very day in spite of much criticism and opposition.

For us today, we must revert back to the original idea of the word "Catholic." The Catholic Church is the whole Church, the entire Church, the total Church. It is all of the believers, not just a few of the believers. The Catholic Church is all who have responded to the call of God. It has its unity in the saving work and grace of Jesus Christ's life, death and resurrection. The Catholic Church is wherever believers are and wherever these believers are submitting their lives to God to let the work of the Holy Spirit come through to the world. The Catholic Church is wherever Jesus Christ is in the hearts of men and women.

Thirdly, we are going to deal with the significance of "Holy." Here we have the area of the Church which has received the most criticism. The same Church which has responded to the love of God is the same Church which fails to feed the poor, help the oppressed, accumulated untold wealth, ignored the cries of those in pain, and even gone to war with its fellow human beings. It is the same Church which has had multiple divisions and even fighting among its members and its factions. These harsh realities are hardly grounds to be called Holy.

There are some who say that those of true faith do not participate in these terrible things. However, this ignores the simple truth that we are still sinners in need of God's love and redemption on a daily basis.

So, in what way is the Church Holy? The Church is Holy only because it is composed of those who have responded to God. This holiness is the work of God not of the body of believers and thus comes only from God. Hans Kung said, "The Church is holy by being called by God in Christ to be in the communion of the faithful, by accepting the call to his service, by being separated from the world and at the same time embraced and supported by his grace" (p. 325).

"This holiness, being the work of God's spirit among men, is not accessible to us or controllable by us, it is not something we see, but something that is revealed to these who in faith open their hearts to the sanctifying Spirit of God" (p. 326). So then it is God who gives Holiness and we are still sinners for sin is allowed to exist by the grace of God.

This Holy Catholic Church is not easily defined. It is made up of persons of faith who are sinners in need of God's love and redemption. They all too often act like sinners.

However, it is also about being changed. Believers are charged with living a Holy life. A great part of that holiness comes in association with God. It is God's holiness that makes the Church Holy. In this, we are charged to act like we are Holy.

Building the Church:
Naive Remarks as a Beginning Pastor in Relationship to Nehemiah

While studying the Old Testament, I became interested in the book of Nehemiah. Part of my interest was my confidence that the book was written by Nehemiah. That confidence was shaken later. I have since regained the confidence that Nehemiah wrote the material. It captures observations about the destruction of Jerusalem that strike me as genuine.

I have read the book of Nehemiah thirty-four times. I attempted several of those readings while I was trying to teach myself French. Reading in French didn't help me learn how to speak the language. However, it did slow me down and kept me from engaging the book superficially.

It is very interesting reading.

Early in my ministry I attempted a sermon on building the Church based on my perceptions of Nehemiah. The reason I had decided to choose to do this is because I feel his story has something in the form of encouragement to say.

The encouragement came both as a warning, beware this could happen to you, and as a reflection on overcoming obstacles.

Because of the sins of the leaders of Judah, the kings rejected the Lord God and turned from Him. This angered God and He brought His wrath upon Jerusalem in the form of rising up the king of the Chaldeans who made war on Judah and he slew the young men, and dealt harshly with the people and took those who survived as servants. The walls of Jerusalem were destroyed and broken down.

It was following this situation that Nehemiah entered the picture. Nehemiah was a cup bearer for King Artaxerxes and they were in Susa the capital of Elam. (Elam was located, in the area which today we call Iraq and

Iran and was north of the Persian Gulf. It was the winter residence of the Persian Kings.).

Sadness of heart was reflected in Nehemiah's role as cup bearer and he was confronted by King Artaxerxes concerning his sad face. The cup bearer for the king was not to have a sad face. However, Nehemiah found the king compassionate.

Nehemiah quickly prayed to God and told the king about the situation at Jerusalem and requested that he be sent to Judah in order that he might rebuild the walls of Jerusalem. The king was pleased to send him and Nehemiah asked for letters to the provinces that he might be able to pass through to Judah with no problem.

However, when he came to the province "Beyond the River", and gave officials the letters, there were some who were displeased that one would be interested in the welfare of the children of Israel.

Nehemiah arrived at Jerusalem and was there for three days. He went out at night taking only one mount and a few men and secretly inspected the walls of the city. He did this so that no one would know what he was doing before he announced his plans to the people. A particular incident on this inspection has often captured my attention. On coming to the Fountain Gate, Nehemiah reported that he and his ride could not pass because of the severe destruction. "And I went out by night by the gate of the valley, even before the dragon well, and to the dung port, and viewed the walls of Jerusalem, which were broken down, and the gates thereof were consumed with fire. Then I went on to the gate of the fountain, and to the king's pool: but there was no place for the beast that was under me to pass" Nehemiah 2:13-14 (KJV).

After inspecting the wall, Nehemiah approached the Jews, the priests, the nobles, the officials, and the rest that were to do the work of rebuilding, and he said to them, "Then said I unto them, Ye see the distress that we are in, how Jerusalem lieth waste, and the gates thereof are burned with fire: come, and let us build up the wall of Jerusalem, that we be no more a reproach" Nehemiah 2:17 (KJV). And Nehemiah let them know that the hand of God was on him and they rose up and started to build the wall.

So, the work on rebuilding the wall began. During the project, those who were displeased with the idea of help for the children of Israel became angered and enraged. They began wondering what it would lead to. As the building continued, these enemies started to plot against Jerusalem to go and wage war on the people. The people became fearful, but Nehemiah set up a plan to guard the city from attack and God frustrated the plan of the enemies of Jerusalem.

There came an outcry of the people. Many were poor. They became poorer because they had to sell what little they had or mortgage what little they had in order to eat. Some became servants in order to eat. When Nehemiah heard of this and heard their cry, he became very angry and asked those who had taken the possessions of the poor to give back those things and to loan money without interest. This was done and the people were pleased.

The wall was finally rebuilt. However, when the enemies of Jerusalem and the children of Israel heard this, they attempted to lure Nehemiah into a trap. Fortunately, they were unsuccessful for he knew what they were trying to do.

When the wall was completed, the people worshiped God and celebrated as commanded, through the Law of Moses. They also offered an agreement and covenant with God to keep His commandments. After doing these things, they offered a dedication of the wall.

So, the story is complete. Well as complete as a brief account from Nehemiah and restating of that account here allows.

Leaping out of Nehemiah's presentation was the opposition to rebuilding the wall. It was external and internal. Yet, despite the threats from outside, the economic crisis inside and the fears of the people, the wall was rebuilt. God did not let anything stand in the way of this work. I am not prepared to speak of the miraculous. Much needed supplies, or construction materials didn't appear out of virtually no where. There are no angels showing up to fend off adversaries. Real human conflict though is overcome and dealt with. Progress was made and the task completed. It is real clear to me that Nehemiah felt and believed that God was very involved in this project.

God provided a leader, a leader who felt strongly about the task. This leader knew God would help with the rebuilding of the wall. He was not afraid or hesitant to call on the Lord God when the occasion arrived and he knew God would heed the call. The leader was so confident of God's help that the workers, who probably were hoping for a leader to guide them in rebuilding the wall, immediately and enthusiastically said, "Yes, let us build the wall." They saw the hand of God was on Nehemiah. That is faith at work in the midst of a down to earth situation. This is where God often works.

Nehemiah working under the power of God stood fast against the opposition. That opposition said "we are not going to let you build the wall." The workers themselves said, "We cannot do it. We are afraid of the opposition."

Though I just wrote that the people believed, it is also clear the opposition came from within as well. The external and internal opposition was overcome. Thus the wall got rebuilt by the people even though they at times did not think it could be done in the face of opposition.

This story reminds me of the situation of a Church. It could be any Church. There may not be any physical desolation or destruction. However, there is always some building to do and some building which has already taken place. A Church may have built a parsonage, but not without opposition. The Church may be afraid, "we cannot do such and such." However, one among the Church members said, "Yes it can be done" and indeed a project got completed. Not only was it built, but paid for in short order.

Building continues. New and old pastors are part of Churches where building is taking place. The Church may have made one step toward with a new project. The step was made in spite of fears. Yet, there may still be disbelief. The sound of "we cannot do it" may resonate. In order to complete a project, the Church has to grow. It is not necessarily numerical growth. The growth may be the growth that comes with facing adversity. The voice of the inner opposition exists. "We cannot grow, there are too many . . . around here (Fill in the gap). There are too many non-Churched people around here. The opposition is probably strong, but the power and Spirit of God is stronger.

We, as a people of faith, grow because God will touch peoples' hearts for us. However, we must do some things. We must trust God as the source, for only He can bring us the growth. Thus, in building a Church, whatever that building is, we must pray to God to touch the hearts of those who can help and want to be a part of the project. Then, we must invite these people (within and without). They are our friends. They are our fellow workers. They are our relatives.

The Struggle To Believe

This day and age is one of those times in which it is extremely hard for people to believe in a personal savior. We are passing through one of the most challenging eras ever faced by the Church as a whole at any time in its history. Book after book, article after article shows the decline in Church in our country and in Europe. Attendance and membership has been in decline in the mainline denominations since I graduated from high school in the late 60s. The Church during this time has been called hypocritical, irrelevant, and apathetic. God was declared dead and also nonexistent. It has been an era marked by a major struggle to believe.

Today people are taking a second look at God and considering agnosticism and atheism. I can see this in the secular world. When I was going to Oglethorpe University in the 70s, I can remember that we did not dare talk conservatively about Jesus without facing belittlement and sarcasm. That has not changed.

I take that back. It has changed. Now, the belittlement and sarcasm is more profound among those who profess to be Christians. I have sat down with non-Church goers, agnostics and atheists and talked about my faith and seen ridicule or sarcasm being strong. I had yet another conversation just a few weeks ago with a "Christian" who ridiculed the Bible and those who took it seriously.

A number of years ago, one of the atheists I talked to almost came to church at my invitation. She a person with whom I talked about religion many times and indicated an interest in seeing what Church had to offer. However, her skepticism was also about Christians, not just their beliefs. Further, she really didn't raise any issues that skeptical Christians are raising. Thus, she couldn't find justification for attending a worship experience.

It needs to be seen that even though people are demonstrating an interest in God. They only talk about it.

However, I believe that many people, with patient invitation, may be on the verge of moving toward God and accepting Jesus Christ's lifesaving work. In the meantime, there is reluctance on their parts to turn to God for salvation and even to believe.

So it is important for us to deal with the struggle to believe.

I can remember when I was in Junior College reading a little pocket addition of Good News for Modern Man New Testament. I was very concerned about the new morality that was developing. Free love was being promoted. There was an increase of drug abuse that was growing and the increase in general disillusionment, confusion, hostility, and frustration being seen in the youth of America. I remember underlining verses in that New Testament which were designed to give comfort, strength, and meaning in life to people. I remember the pain in my heart for my peers as I saw them desperately searching for meaning, but rejecting the very concepts which would give meaning, namely Jesus as the Christ. I kept saying to myself, "if only they would accept Jesus, their lives would turn around. They could find joy and peace and the love for which they so desperately yearned.

However, it wasn't that easy. There were too many forces in life which made it difficult to trust in God instead of themselves. And unfortunately these forces still exist today and have to be reckoned with by the believers if we are to help people come to faith in Jesus Christ. One of these is our affluence. Another is psychology. And then there are sociological forces. Finally, there is the intellectual or more specifically the scientific forces.

Affluence

One of the major forces which makes it difficult for us to believe, is our affluence. On a day to day basis we simply do not need God. We have plenty to eat. We have plenty to drink.

We have good housing facilities. We have the best medical care available in the world and thus do not need to face long existing medical problems, such as small pox, plague, diphtheria, and the like. We are able to travel great distances in a short period of-time. In short, we have all the basic necessities in life and our only real discontentment is that we cannot always get what we want in luxury items. When we have difficulties, it is often because we are over extended. When tough economic times occur, we have trouble making ends meet.

Therefore we do not need God to look out after the basic necessities in life. We get these by working for them and buying them from each other. Our materialism is our god.

Psychology

Another force which makes it difficult for us to believe is psychology. Psychology offers several interpretations of religious phenomenon. I will only mention them and not discuss them here. Two important thinkers in this come to mind, Sigmund Freud and Albert Ellis.

One of the interpretations is we have to believe in God because of our fear of the unknown. God is simply a way of explaining away the things we do not understand. Another is we use religion to repress the basic drives which come in conflict with sociological expectations. Yet another is that our religion is an effort on our part to create a source for something to meet our needs for the love of a father and the love of a mother.

These are just a couple of the ideas from psychology which can help ignore the reality of God by trying to show us that our concept of God is of our own making. They completely reject that there very well may be a God who is revealing himself to a world which may be incapable of recognizing him.

Sociological

There are sociological forces which make it difficult for us to believe in God. I am not as familiar with the concepts available and can think of only two. Peer pressure is one. The other is Marxism.

Peer pressure has the strongest effect on us. In our day and age people tend to look down on getting up and going to Church. We think it rests in us that we see Church as irrelevant, boring, and unimportant. These are common perceptions in our society that have influenced peoples' perceptions. In this, it is simply better to sleep late, or go to the lake than to worship God. In order to stay away from worship we have rationalized away God as described earlier or in a similar manner.

The Marxist statement on religion is less threatening to us. Most people don't even think about it. They may not even know it exists. Nevertheless, it is a notion that makes it difficult for us to believe in God. Marx simply said that religion is the opium of the people. What he meant by this is the upper class (bourgeois) used religion to pacify the lower class (proletariat) so they would not rebel against their oppression. There is enough of us people in the world today who are suspicious enough to buy this concept even if unconsciously and thus not believe in God. Religion in the absence of the old Marxist notions of bourgeois, and proletariat is actually about elitism, the well-off suppressing the naive or oppressed with the pacifism of religion.

Science

Finally, there are scientific forces which make it difficult for us to believe. Darwin gets too much credit for leading us astray from God. He pulled from an already existing intellectual scientific community which influenced him a great deal. It just organized the ideals in such a way that they appealed to the masses. Somehow, he became popular when others saying the same things went unnoticed. It is doubtful he said anything that was really new.

Natural selection is often singled out in relationship to Darwin's theory. However, it really doesn't offer an explanation of how creatures adapt and change physically so they can actually be in a position to be coincidentally selected by the forces of nature.

I am convinced that concepts of the actualization tendency or organization tendency would be better suited to explain evolution than Darwin's materials.

That aside, evolution and other scientific principles have made it difficult to believe in a creator who made all which exists. The Big Bang theory of the beginning of the universe makes it hard to believe in God the creator. Maybe not as much as a theory, but by virtue of all those who believe in it.

Genetics also has thrown some bones in the ring to confuse us. Biochemistry really has us backed up against the wall with its being used to making life possible.

So in the face of all these things, how do we come to believe? We come to believe by using the very same forces which supposedly can blind us to God's existence. Dare we use the very forces that inhibit or discourage belief?

First, we can believe in God through our affluence. Second, we can believe in God through our psychology. Third, we can believe in God through our sociology. Finally, we can believe in God through science.

Affluence

First, we can believe in God through our affluence. We can reflect on James' observation. "Every good gift and every perfect gift is from above, and cometh down from the Father of lights, with whom is no variableness, neither shadow of turning" James 1:17 (KJV).

I stated earlier in this chapter that in our affluence we do not need God. However, when we get behind the gift of affluence and see what we have, we must realize that we do indeed need God even though we are affluent. If there is no God, from the standpoint of faith, there would be no affluence and there would be no existence. The elements we use to meet our basic needs exist because of God's creative hand and because of God's love. So all the good things we have come from God.

In addition, the Old Testament has numerous stories of people blessed of God and being affluent by the standards of their time. From Abraham, to David, to the nation of Israel itself, affluence was a mark of being blessed of God while keeping the faith.

Psychology

Second, we can believe in God through our psychology. I really feel that all the different schools of psychology are more evidence of the desperateness of the human situation. By studying psychology, it is extremely difficult to assimilate all there is to understand and then it is found out that life's situations are unchanged. There is as much pain and suffering and the like in the world as ever before, and psychology has not changed a thing. If anything, it has made matters worse by adding to the confusion. A colleague and friend of mine who was an atheist and who believed profoundly in the goodness of human beings said not long before she died, "This world is going to hell." She was completely dismayed by the deterioration of the human condition and society even though she made significant contributions to the theoretical and practical approach to psychotherapy she valued the most.

So, can this not be interpreted to show we need a God to deliver us from our problems and then can we not look at Jesus Christ to see that this is just what happened for us? If psychology verifies the troubles of human kind, its brokenness, estrangement, and alienation from each other, it does verify some of the claims about sin. Human beings need help. In faith, we assert we get it in the form of the life, death, and resurrection of Jesus Christ.

Sociology

Third, we can believe in God through our sociology. As we study the societies of the world we find that every people have had a concept of God. Recently at a study involving ministers of different denominations one of the participants asked, "What do you all do about the people of other societies and cultures who have faith, but don't believe in Jesus Christ." He saved that complex question to the end of the meeting. One of the clergy members responded, "I have enough trouble getting Christians to be Christians without trying to deal with people of other faiths." My own question to the question is, "If these people have so much faith and that faith is of God, why do they reject Jesus as the Christ? Why don't they at least embrace Jesus as the Christ?" It reminds me of Jethro and Moses in the desert during the Exodus event where Jethro, a man of faith who had many gods, recognized what God did for Moses and the people of Israel (Exodus 18).

So why can we not interpret this to mean that the reason most every people thinks in terms of the existence of God is that He is revealing Himself to the world. It is just as sensible to believe this as it is to believe in an abstract idea like people believe in God because of their fear of the unknown.

I remember a lunch conversation I had with a female counseling colleague where the discussion came around to religion. She told me she believed all paths lead to God. I told her that I don't believe all paths lead to God, but that I have room for the one that does being interpreted and perceived differently. Surely, there are paths that don't lead to God. And surely, God could, would, and did find a way to reveal Himself to the world.

Once Jesus is understood as the Christ, why does a person need another perspective on the path revealed by God? If there is a need for these other paths or interpretations, I assert that Jesus is not the Christ.

I digressed, but that peoples have believed in God, or gods through the ages leaves me with evidence that there is revelation behind these beliefs even if they are wrong or disagree.

Science

Finally, we can believe in God through science. Wernher Von Braun, the late former head of our efforts to put people into space, allegedly commented many times that when he looked at the complexity of the universe he could not help but believe in God. Are not any such remarks similar to Paul's words:

"For the invisible things of him from the creation of the world are clearly seen, being understood by the things that are made, even his eternal power and Godhead; so that they are without excuse" Romans 1:20 (KJV). When we look at life and realize that life can only come from life, we have to look at a life giving creator as the source of life to make life possible.

And so through observation of science, we can believe in God. We do not find God in the test tube, the microscope, the telescope, the computer, or mathematical formulas. Instead, we find complexity that is suggestive of a creative hand. With all our own creativity, we have yet to create our own complexity. Yet, here in this obscure place in a vast universe something different exists, life. The Bible and faith point to a creator.

There is evidence for both sides of believing and not believing. So it is a matter of what would you prefer to believe. We have an opportunity to believe and explore the evidence for God. Faith is the basis of that belief.

The Search For Faith

In the last chapter, "The Struggle to Believe," I tried to show that there are significant forces in the world which make it difficult for us to believe in God. I also tried to show that these same forces can also help us believe. This essentially leaves us with the choice to believe or not to believe. My own world is a mix of believers and nonbelievers though primarily I relate most often to believers. I often hear a question. What is the difference between believers and nonbelievers? It certainly isn't that we as believers are better. We do claim to be more enlightened, but this enlightenment we claim is not of ourselves. Nonbelievers also claim to be more enlightened. However, this enlightenment is not of ourselves. So what is the difference?

It is faith. So in this chapter, there is an exploration faith. It will hardly be exhaustive.

Before exploring faith, I want to look at a misconception about faith. There are those who have heard that faith is like sitting down on a chair. We have faith as we have time and time again sat in chairs. We have done this so often that we come to believe they will, in all likelihood, hold us up. We often do not even think about it, we just sit down in them.

Occasionally though a chair tips with us or breaks. However, it is rare enough that we do not have conscious concern about the chair failing to hold our weight. This is supposed to be called faith.

However, there are major problems with this analogy. Sitting in a chair is a very concrete event. We can see and feel on a sensory level most every aspect of our action. We also can draw from the repetition of the action that each time we sit down in a chair we are successfully held up. We also have a sense of intellect which helps look at the chair and determine if it is sturdy enough to hold us. We also have a sense of balance which can help us with a fall if we do happen to misjudge the chair. And, we also know that if these fail and we do fall we do not have far to fall.

This is not faith, because we have the ability to make a judgment concerning the chair and see ourselves in relationship with the chair.

We do not have the ability to see God and our relationship to him for we are sinners, lost and separated from and blind to God. Faith therefore is not as instantaneous as sitting in a chair.

The Lord works on us in many ways before we finally see the light. And then there are stills times of doubt, fear, anxiety, frustration, and discouragement. We know at once when we see people sitting in chairs that the chair in which we will sit will more than likely hold us up as well, and after the first time we know that chairs support. This is not so with faith. We cannot see faith in others for we see people with faith. They are fearful, anxious, frustrated and discouraged also. We see different degrees of faith. People have different levels of trusting God and even starting out on different levels of trusting God. This is confusing to us and makes it harder to come to grips with faith.

So let us investigate briefly what faith is.

Let us start off first by exploring what faith is. In order to do this it is imperative that we turn to scripture to define faith. Here is what can be found. The best definition that can be seen in scripture concerning faith is found in the letter attributed to Paul called Hebrews.

In Hebrews 11:1 we see the following words: "Now faith is the substance of things hoped for, the evidence of things not seen" Hebrews 11:1 (KJV). There are two things we need to see here. Faith is something hoped for. It is also the conviction of things unseen.

The ESV translates the first part: "Faith is the assurance of things hoped for." It is confidence in the things hoped for. We cannot say that it is a knowledge of things which is similar to the knowledge of things we can see with our eyes, or smell with our nose, or taste with our mouth, or feel with our tactile sensations, or hear with our ears. However, faith is a kind of knowing. It is a spiritual experience.

I think what is often missed in this is not seeing through our physical senses, it's that this knowledge is about "things hoped for." Such things include love, grace, peace, and joy to name a few. Certainly included in this would be that Jesus Christ has been raised from the dead, and given the gift of eternal life. Neither of these has been seen by any believer today.

We have awareness that God is going to deliver us. We trust that God has redeemed us. We cannot prove it through scientific or human methodologies. We step into a spiritual paradigm instead.

The assurance in this model comes with the life, death, and resurrection making sense. It is not an opinion. It is grasping the Jesus event with similar belief that George Washington was the first president of the United States. The Jesus event is that real.

Faith is also the conviction of things not seen. We are not dealing with something we can see with our eyes, hear with our ears, or feel by touch. We are dealing with things that are unseen. However, through faith we begin to see and hear and feel. We start to understand and comprehend and thus develop a conviction concerning that which is unseen by the visual eye and the audible ear. Somehow, we feel we are aware of God's presence and sometimes feel he is right beside us and talking to us.

This sounds almost cut and dried, but it is not. Faith on a conscious level seems to be very elusive. As I have already said, we may experience doubt, fear, anxiety, frustration, and discouragement. These are not all the things which cause us to question our faith or make us wonder if we really do believe.

I think the best example of a person struggling with faith is the Methodist founding father, John Wesley. So let us briefly explore him. Those who investigate Wesley quickly note that he struggled with his faith. He had a doubt that caused him a lot of anguish. We can see this again and again in his writings especially in his early writings.

On Wesley's trip home to England from America, he knew he was going to have to report and live with his failure as a minister here in this country. We see one of the occasions where he struggles with his faith in his journal. He wrote in January of 1738 the following: "By the most infallible of proofs, in word feeling I am convinced:

1. Of unbelief - having no such faith in Christ as will prevent my heart from being troubled, which it could not be, if I believed in God, and rightly believed also in Him" (Wesley, 1997, p. 87). At a later date Wesley wrote: "I went to America, to convert the Indians; but O! who shall convert me? who, what is he that will deliver me from this evil heart of unbelief? I have a fair summer religion. I can talk well; nay, and believe myself, while no danger is near: But let death look me in the face, and my spirit is troubled" (p. 90). And again Wesley wrote: "The faith I want is, a sure trust and confidence in God, that, through the merits of Christ, my sins are forgiven, and I reconciled to the favor of God. I want that faith which St. Paul recommends to all the world,

especially in his Epistle to the Romans, that faith which enables everyone that hath it to cry out: 'I live not; but Christ liveth in me; and the life which I now live, I live by faith in the Son of God, who loved me and gave himself for me.' I want that faith which none can have without knowing he hath it; (though many imagine they have it, who have it not;) for whosoever hath it, is 'freed from sin the' whole 'body of sin is destroyed' in him; He is freed from fear, 'having peace with God through Christ and rejoicing in hope of the glory of God.' And he is freed from doubt, 'having the love of God shed abroad in his heart, through the Holy Ghost which is given unto him;' which 'Spirit itself beareth witness with his spirit that he is a child of God'" (p. 92-93). So we see Wesley's struggle with his faith. It is rather profound as it is not what we expect from a religious leader.

On the other hand, we have John Calvin and nowhere have I ever seen anything which describes Calvin's doubt. Of course, this does not mean that he did not have doubt. It may not be available to the general public. O to his followers. At any rate, Calvin is one who would he considered to have had a strong and confident faith.

Now, the next question we need to consider is how do we get a strong faith? And frankly, I must say I do not know the specific answer to this question if what Wesley held as strong faith is the standard. I have possibilities with which I work. I would not say that any one of them is the way to strong faith. However, I will stick my neck out and point to that which is the most important way of getting faith.

We get faith through God. God is the giver of faith. Without Him, without an encounter with Him, there could not be faith. Apart from His life, love, and work there cannot be faith. Faith is the gift of God and is given to people so they can choose to respond to God, if they so desire. Thus faith, or certainly an encounter may be something that everyone has, but many refuse to accept. At any rate, it would make sense if you want to be strong and confident in faith, ask God for faith and do not reject what he gives you.

Now you say you have asked for and have not received faith. Then there are some other ways one is supposed to get faith. It seems that we allow Satan to blind us to the truth of God's love and salvation and thus we do not have faith. The way to a stronger faith is to realize that we let Satan blind us to the truth and by letting Satan blind us, we do not have to take the responsibility for our lack of faith and can say Satan blinded us. Then by realizing that we let this happen, we can move toward a stronger faith by admitting we are the sinners who are letting Satan blind us. When we do this, we take the responsibility for our blindness and can then see the light and allow God to give us more faith. Personally, I tend to think the Satan argument is the weakest as it gives the devil too much credit and power.

Also, I think lack of faith walks hand in hand with insecurity. We just do not believe we are important enough to be loved by God. So we, in our lowly place, reject notions of God's existence. We then do not have to be lifted up from our insecurity. We can wallow around in our insecurity. It strikes me that there is a certain amount of security in being insecure for at least we are familiar with that kind of life. Security can be found in familiarity. However, if we want a stronger faith, then we need to realize we are creatures of God whom God loved enough to deliver from our alienation and separation.

Another part of this insecurity comes with not believing our eyes. God does neat things on our behalf and we don't believe it. Obviously, the most significant example of not believing what God has put before us is the life, death, and resurrection of Jesus Christ.

There is a joke about not believing our eyes. During a severe flood a man was stranded on the roof top of his house. A man with a boat came by and offered to rescue him. The man turned him down saying that God would rescue him. A little later, a helicopter came and he was offered another rescue. He turned that down.

The flood waters continued to rise and he was swept away and drowned. At the pearly gates the man asked St. Peter why God didn't rescue him. St. Peter said, "God sent you a row boat and a helicopter. You didn't take either of them."

Again, God sent His son Jesus Christ. Many refuse to accept this gesture and look for another path. It is well known that in that effort there are many who assert all paths lead to God. This in itself is problematic on several fronts. It says there are no paths that lead away from God. It undermines Jesus as the Christ by saying other paths work. If Jesus is the Christ then why are other paths needed. If other paths are sufficient, why does the world need Jesus at all?

Concreteness In Faith

The past two chapters have been concerned with the forces which keep us from having faith and also help us have faith. Faith was defined according to scriptural statements of faith. The primary one was: "Now faith is the substance of things hoped for, the evidence of things not seen" Hebrews 11:1 (KJV).

In the previous efforts, Wesley's struggle to believe was presented. Suggestions were also offered concerning some things to help us have a stronger faith.

In this chapter, I want to deal with the concreteness of faith. By this I mean those concrete issues which have to be ignored or rationalized away in order not to believe. They will be things we can see or hear. First, there is the existence of life. Second, there is scripture. Third, there is tradition. Lastly, there is Jesus Christ.

The Existence of Life

Here I know the arguments of the Big Bang Theory and evolution place grave questions on the existence of life being started by a God. However, I have to go along with Werhner Von Braun when he said that when he looked at the universe and its complexity, he had to believe in God. In examining the existence of life in relation to this universe, we have not found concrete evidence to say life exists elsewhere in the universe. We also have not found a means of starting life from mere chemicals. Any efforts and accomplishments made toward test tube life have been made from chemicals coming from living material. There is thus no serious challenge to the biological law which says life comes only from life. If this observable data is not a mistake, it is logical that if there is a beginning to life, then life came from a living force. This suggests a life giver, a creator, namely God. There is nothing illogical about this and the logic gives concreteness to faith in a creator who is responsible for the existence of life.

There are several scriptural references which I would like to share with you that are concerned with the universe and the creator:

"For the invisible things of him from the creation of the world are clearly seen, being understood by the things that are made, even his eternal power and Godhead; so that they are without excuse" Romans 1:20 (KJV).

"I will lift up mine eyes unto the hills, from whence cometh my help. My help cometh from the LORD, which made heaven and earth" Psalm 121:1-2 (KJV).

"Where wast thou when I laid the foundations of the earth? declare, if thou hast understanding. Who hath laid the measures thereof, if thou knowest? or who hath stretched the line upon it? Whereupon are the foundations thereof fastened? or who laid the corner stone thereof; When the morning stars sang together, and all the sons of God shouted for joy?" Job 38:4-7 (KJV).

This not quantum physics, it is the concreteness of faith. It rests in part what can be seen. However, it also rests in what cannot be seen. Chief among the unseen is God and God's creative hand.

Scripture

This leads to the second concrete aspect of faith, Scripture. Here we find that which we can see and hear and this gives concreteness to faith. I am familiar with the arguments against scripture being the Word of God. I am not a walking encyclopedia on these arguments. I can say I have heard them time and time again over the years. Sometimes I get sick and tired of hearing them. However, since questions concerning the validity and accuracy of scripture exist, they have to be recognized as existing. I do revisit such questions regularly.

I'd like to say there are some absolutely unquestionable parts of scripture. I can't say that because every aspect of scripture has been discarded by somebody. Yet, many aspects of life are questionable. When events and experiences are seen through different eyes, differences of views lead people to question the observations of others. Anyway, I believe there is a lot of scripture which has as firm a foundation to stand upon as any other historical document. I want to deal with a couple of these.

While I was in my first year of seminary, I was taking a course of introduction to the Old Testament. I was struggling trying to find something concrete to grasp. The historical validity of the Old Testament even more than the New Testament has received much more convincing challenges concerning its accuracy.

Anyway, I was looking at the prophets trying to find something recognized as true prophecy and not something recognized as being written after an event or events it was supposed to be predicting. I found what I was looking for with the little book of Nahum. So, I wrote a paper about it. I did a lousy of job on it and only got a C for my efforts. However, I would like to share some of what I found.

The only thing we know about Nahum the prophet is that he was associated with a place called Elkosh. The location of Elkosh is unkown. Thus there is little value here for us regarding information. It probably doesn't really matter where Nahum had his roots. It has been speculated that it may have been a little village in Galilee known as Elkesi. Nahum himself is not known for other sources of Old Testament literature or writings. The date of the writing has been placed by Oxford Annotated Bible as a period between 626 B.C. and 612 B.C. being the time when the city of Ninevah mentioned in the book was destroyed. There are scholars who seem to feel positive the book was indeed written shortly before Ninevah's fall.

Nahum wrote his words in reaction to the beginning of the decline of the powerful Assyrian Empire. This empire ruled an area from Mesopotamia to the Mediterranean. About 630 B.C., the decline started following the death of Ashurbanipal king of the Assyrians. Invasions by the Medes to the north of Persia and the Chaldeans of south Babylonia were principal reasons for the fall of this empire that subjected the Hebrews to its power.

The book is concerned with expressing the reaction to the overthrow of Assyria and tells of the coming destruction of Ninevah. Ninevah was to fall because "it is the Lord's judgment upon an unscrupulous, defiant nation" (May & Metzger, 1965, p. 1132). Nahum felt this destruction was inevitable. The Assyrian Empire was getting what it deserved for its unjust actions of oppression of people and rejection of God.

In the book of prophecy by Nahum, we find as concrete evidence as is available under any incident in the history of the world. Granted there are a lot of questions about the book of Nahum. However, there are significant questions related to every topic examined by human beings. That is not grounds to discard the significance of works. Thus Nahum remains to be dealt with as a work of scripture.

Another portion of scripture which offers us strong support is the Gospel of Luke. Like many things in life there are many significant questions that arise concerning Luke's work. Still, we have in Luke a work of an intelligent human being who was obviously struck by the significance of the events about which he was writing. Luke wrote: "Forasmuch as many have taken in hand to set forth in order a declaration of those things which are most surely believed among us, even as they delivered them unto us, which from the beginning were eyewitnesses, and ministers of the word; It seemed good to me also, having had perfect understanding of all things from the very first, to write unto thee in order, most excellent Theophilus, That thou mightest know the certainty of those things, wherein thou hast been instructed" Luke 1:1-4 (KJV)

We see from this introduction to Luke that the writer of this work used other narratives. It is widely held that Mark was one of these sources (Marshall, 1978). I have tried to wiggle around that unsuccessfully for years feeling that Mark, in its brevity, was written after Luke and Matthew. Luke used eyewitness accounts with speculations being that Mary, Jesus' mother, was one of these. I have long since forgotten where I got hold of that claim. That does not mean these eyewitness accounts were the result of Luke's own interactions with those sources. He drew from his own experience and exposure to the events or accounts about which he wrote even if secondhand. If this is the Luke associated with Paul, he should have had access to information about events or accounts. If he found them worth considering, he would have included them. Marshall (1978) asserts there are style differences in material unique to Luke. Is it unreasonable to think these differences are in part attributed to access to different resources? This work is not a haphazard effort done by some sort of fanatic. Luke developed this very carefully in order to make sure he presented the best available material to bring to the forefront the truth of the things which had been accomplished. We therefore can trust Luke, he was not writing about a personal fantasy or illusion. He was writing about was given to him over the years. It is not material he has made up in order to deceive the reader. It is material with which he has had a personal relationship. He knew what he was writing about was, is, and will continue to be true.

Tradition

The third thing which gives us concreteness in faith is tradition. The good news of the gospels has been handed down from generation to generation. A certain amount of concreteness is found in the reality that from generation to generation people have accepted the good news. It has made sense to new generations. Usually, only truth survives the test of time because people search for truth and tend to find out about the things which are reliable and which are not. It may take some time to make discoveries that make the reliability issues clearer. However, our tradition has been under examination for nearly 2000 years. While it has been rejected by many, it has also been espoused by many.

Part of this concreteness in tradition is it is made up of people who have responded to God's message. The fact that there is a body of believers suggests there is reality to the notion that God acted in history, is acting in history, and will continue to act in history. The Church then gives reality and validity to the historical events which occurred two thousand years ago.

Jesus Christ

Finally, Jesus Christ gives us concreteness for faith. In Jesus Christ, we have a historical figure. He was a person who lived and breathed and talked. He surrounded himself with people. We are thus dealing with a historical reality. Our faith is based on this historical reality. Without the history we would not have this faith and there is concreteness in this. Without the history, we would not have this faith. Since we have this historical reality in Jesus Christ, we can say our faith is reality and is well founded. I personally find it valuable that there are those who question the historical basis of our faith. The questioning, though it used to trouble me, adds validity to the basis of faith.

References

Marshall, I. H. (1978). Commentary on Luke: New International Greek Testament Commentary. Grand Rapids, MI: William B. Eerdmans Publishing Company.

May, H. G., & Metzger, B. M. (Eds). (1965). The Oxford annotated Bible with the Apocrypha. New York, NY: Oxford University Press.

Repentance For
The Forgiveness Of Sins

In one of my classes in seminary we made a study of Luke 3:1ff. The section deals with John the Baptist and his ministry in the region of the Jordan. We were thinking in terms of its significance and I noticed that his preaching for repentance for the forgiveness of sins was concerned with three basic concepts. First, there was the conviction of Sin in order to be freed from its bonds. Second, the freedom from sin will enable us to live a more righteous life. Third, with repentance there is the hope there is even more to come. This more, is not limited to a future of righteous behavior and any blessings that come with it. It also is about eternal life.

In this chapter, I want to deal with repentance for the forgiveness of sins as I perceive it to have been preached by John the Baptist.

Conviction

First, there is the conviction of sin in order to be freed from its bonds. In saying this, there is a paradoxical experience, one is convicted of sin to be liberated from it, but it remains a reality. The Baptist said, "to the multitude that came forth to be baptized of him, O generation of vipers, who hath warned you to flee from the wrath to come? Bring forth therefore fruits worthy of repentance, and begin not to say within yourselves. We have Abraham to our father: for I say unto you, That God is able of these stones to raise up children unto Abraham. And now also the axe is laid unto the root of the trees: every tree therefore which bringeth not forth good fruit is hewn down, and cast into the fire" Luke 3:7-9 (KJV).

What strikes me about the conviction of sins is the harshness John used. There is condemnation and judgment. He was firm and tough with his words. He made no bones about people being sinners needing to turn from their ways and begin to lead a new life.

As a preacher, I am reluctant to capture some of that. I have found the judgmental model difficult. Traditionally preaching concerning repentance has either been full of bitterness and hostility toward sinners or too wishy-washy. It seems to me, we need to find a way to communicate an awareness of sinfulness. In some ways, we have to find a position between the bitterness and the wishy-washiness that is designed to convict people of their sins.

I really believe the key to the conviction of sin lies deeper than efforts to point out wrong doing. Wrong doing or bad behavior is really a symptom of our sinfulness. We are persons who are lost, blind to, and separated from God. We are corrupted, rebellious, and resistant to God's authority. Therefore, we try to do our own thing and, as a result of our efforts to run the show, we fail again and again. A "doctrine of unintended consequences" was noted by Robert K. Merton in the 20th Century. It essentially asserted that human actions and behavior may trigger unintended adverse consequences. For instance, psychiatric medicine for depression has been connected with suicide and certain more often with side effects such as allergic reactions. While we search for joy, behaviors that had been previously been forbidden such as promiscuity and homosexuality have increased. As they are now defended and justified as viable human choices, tension exists in society. Criticism of these behaviors has been viewed as facilitating hate crimes. Divorce and broken relationships continue to increase as we search for self esteem. As we make tremendous technological advances, pollution and wastefulness increase as we search for happiness through our progress. The world often sits on the verge of World War III as we search for security.

By thrusting ourselves deeply into the impact or reality of sin, we get our conviction of sin. We can thus begin to see in our blindness. We can begin to cooperate with God in our resistance. This moves us to seeing the sin and its devastation. We see how overwhelming it is.

But how do we come to see? This is accomplished only by listening to the witness of the Holy Spirit in our lives. Only God can provide the light for us to see in our darkness. Even then, we resist and reject God's revelation all too often. The Holy Spirit is there witnessing to us in our blindness. "Behold, I stand at the door, and knock: if any man hear my voice, and open the door, I will come in to him, and will sup with him, and he with me" Revelation 3:20 (KJV).

When we acknowledge that presence in our lives, when we heed that call for our lives, then we become convicted of our sins. When we become convicted of our sins, we are starting on the way toward real living through God's all-knowing sovereign way. That way is not going to mislead us but help us to lead a full, meaningful life. When we are finally convicted of sin, we can finally be freed from the bond of sin. We can thus begin to move on to a life style which recognizes God as the source of life and knowledge. Then we can begin to really live as free persons who can have true peace, joy, happiness, and security.

A word of caution needs to be inserted here. We must not get caught up in the theology which says if we only accept Jesus Christ as our personal savior, then we will have a life of bliss. This kind of theology fails to recognize that through experiences of peace, joy, and love reflect the impact of faith, we are still sinners in need of God's love and redemption every moment of our lives. We are thus subject to making mistakes, and in some cases awful decisions which come back to haunt us. We might have disaster experiences that fall outside our control. Something of the life we lived before a confrontation with God remains. Sin also by the grace of God is still a part of our lives. So, there is an element of incompleteness that I associate with eschatology and which I will discuss briefly shortly.

Freedom

Second, the freedom to experience grace, though sin remains, enables us to live a more righteous or holy life. Once we are convicted of sin, we are then freed to obey God. We therefore can begin to live a life similar to what John the Baptist instructed the multitudes to live. "And the people asked him, saying, What shall we do then? He answereth and saith unto them, He that hath two coats, let him impart to him that hath none; and he that hath meat, let him do likewise. Then came also publicans to be baptized, and said unto him, Master, what shall we do? And he said unto them, Exact no more than that which is appointed you. And the soldiers likewise demanded of him, saying, And what shall we do? And he said unto them, Do violence to no man, neither accuse any falsely; and be content with your wages" Luke 3:10-14 (KJV). We can start loving our neighbors as ourselves and doing unto others as we would have them do unto us. We can begin to live the life that God knows will be meaningful.

I think here we come face to face with John Wesley's teachings concerning Christian Perfection. "And loving God, he 'loves his neighbor as himself;' he loves every man as his own soul. He loves his enemies, yea, and the enemies of God. And if it be not; in his power to 'do good to them that hate' him, yet he ceases not to 'pray for them,' though they spurn his love, and still 'despitefully use him, and persecute him'" (Wesley, 1996, p. 434). In this state of faith, we now grow in concern for others by taking care of the sick, visiting the sick, providing for health care, visiting prisoners, establishing facilities for education, and by providing care and facilities for the elderly. We also begin to love God with all our hearts and minds and strength and souls. It is an individual experience and especially a community experience since not all individuals will carry out the same behaviors of grace.

I often wonder how we can continue to neglect others after we have experienced God's Grace. It would seem that having experienced God's love, we would have to follow his instructions because we would know it is the best way to live. I think at times we should not be able to live another way other than to follow him as he says, "If ye love me, keep my commandments" John 14:15 (KJV). It really seems to make sense that after being exposed to the power of grace and love that we should want to share it and that it should radiate out to the world.

Eternal Life

Lastly, with repentance there is the hope that there is even more to come. "And as the people were in expectation, and all men mused in their hearts of John, whether he were the Christ, or not; John answered, saying unto them all, I indeed baptize you with water; but one mightier than I cometh, the latchet of whose shoes I am not worthy to unloose: he shall baptize you with the Holy Ghost and with fire: Whose fan is in his hand, and he will thoroughly purge his floor, and will gather the wheat into his garner; but the chaff he will burn with fire unquenchable" Luke 3:15-17 (KJV). Though verse 17 ends with a negative twist, John the Baptist offers hope that there is more to come. There is more to come even though a lot has been done. Beyond being convicted of our sins and being freed from those sins, and beyond living a more righteous and holy life, there is more to life. The Christ is to come again and eternal life is promised.

Now granted our position today is different than it was for John the Baptist's hearers. The Christ had not yet made his appearance to them.

However, even though the Christ has made his appearance for us, in a sense he is still unseen by us. The coming of the Messiah was to be the ushering in of the Kingdom of God. This is what the Baptist's hearers were expecting. For us, the Kingdom of God has come in one sense. It is represented in the life, death, and resurrection of Jesus Christ. It is also represented in the presence of the Church as created by the Holy Spirit giving people grounds to believe.

In another sense it has not yet arrived. "For, behold, I create new heavens and a new earth: and the former shall not be remembered, nor come into mind" Isaiah 65:17 (KJV). Therefore, just as the hearers of the Baptist had their expectations, we have our expectations that the Lord God Almighty is going to come in his Glory with the return of Christ. when this occurs "every knee shall bow to me, and every tongue shall confess to God" Romans 14:11 (KJV). "For finding fault with them, he saith, Behold, the days come, saith the Lord, when I will make a new covenant with the house of Israel and with the house of Judah: Not according to the covenant that I made with their fathers in the day when I took them by the hand to lead them out of the land of Egypt; because they continued not in my covenant, and I regarded them not, saith the Lord. For this is the covenant that I will make with the house of Israel after those days, saith the Lord; I will put my laws into their mind, and write them in their hearts: and I will be to them a God, and they shall be to me a people: And they shall not teach every man his neighbor, and every man his brother, saying, Know the Lord: for all shall know me, from the least to the greatest" Hebrews 8:8-11 (KJV)

So this is the hope found in repentance for the forgiveness of sins. Hope is an element of repentance which seems to be a must. Without hope there is no reason to repent. If life is to remain as it is and end, then there is absolutely no reason for repentance. However, if life is going to change and continue forever, then by all means we should repent. We should repent based on the hope we see in Christ. For, even though we may not see any significant changes now, we certainly can see significant changes ahead for us in the future through the hope of the reality of the Kingdom of God.

The significance of repentance for the forgiveness of sins does not rest alone with a "turn around" in our lives. Rather, the significance of the repentance for the forgiveness of sins lies in our being convicted of our sin so we can be freed from its bonds in order to live a more righteous and holy life. There is in this a hope that one day the Christ is going to return and the Kingdom of God will be set up. Life will be the way it should be.

References

Wesley, J. (1996). A Plain Account of Christian Perfection: As Believed and Taught by the Reverend Mr. John Wesley, from the Year 1725, to the Year 1777. In the Complete Works of John Wesley, Volume 11, Thoughts, Addresses, Prayers, Letters. The Ages Digital Library Collections. Albany, OR: Books for the Ages, Ages Software, version 2.0.

Wesley, J. (1997). The works of John Wesley, Volume 1: Journals, Oct. 14, 1735 - Nov. 29, 1745. In the Ages Digital Library: collected Works: books for the ages. Albany, OR: Ages software, version 1.0.

How Then Ought We To Live?

We are living in a very ethically and morally challenging age. We have been in a particular sense the baby boomer started getting out of college. Rightly we protested behaving certain ways because we are supposed to like holding prejudices against people who are different. Wrongly by promoting free love and sex outside of marriage. We hear things like "if it feels good do it," or "do your own thing," or "what's wrong with it?" We are now struggling over abortion and homosexuality. Churches are leaving the Episcopalian denomination over the issue of same sex marriage. There has been an increase in promiscuity running rampant in societies around the world. Even church going Christians practice living together and being puzzled when engaged about the issue.

The extremely high rate of divorce in this cynical age continues with homosexuals demanding to get into the traditional institution of marriage that many heterosexuals avoid or attempt to get out of. There is a tremendous amount of corruption in our political leaders.

So, in the face of all this, how then ought we live?

First, we must do unto others as we would have them do unto us. Second, we must love our neighbor as ourselves. Third, we must love our enemies. Finally, we must love God with all our heart and mind and soul and strength.

Do Unto Others

First, we must do unto others as we would have them do unto us. We have heard this all of our lives and found it of great value to try to live up to this. Each of us probably can remember times when we heard this wisdom coming from our parents or other adults while we were growing up. We probably can think of some stories pertaining to doing unto others as we would have them do unto us.

In April 2011, I saw some footage about a softball player in a college tournament who hit a home run during the championship series. It was her only home run ever. As she circled the bases, she realized while she was heading into second base that she had missed first. She abruptly reversed her direction and collapsed in pain. She had torn her ACL in her knee. She crawled back to first base.

As she lay on the ground, her coach checking on her asked the umpire if a pinch runner could take her place. The umpire said yes, but it wouldn't be a home run. The coach then asked if her teammates could help her. The umpire said, no, the player would have to come out of the game.

The star player for the other team then asked if members of the opposing team could carry the young woman around the bases and allow her to touch each base. The umpires could not think of a rule that prohibited it. So two of the opposing team's players picked up the injured player and carried her around the base paths. They helped her put her left foot on each base including home.

The injured player's team won the championship. However, the player was profoundly moved by the opponent's gesture of good will.

We can see some good examples in the teachings found in scripture, when John the Baptist was preaching and preparing the way for Jesus, he was asked about how one should live.

"And the people asked him, saying, What shall we do then? He answereth and saith unto them, He that hath two coats, let him impart to him that hath none; and he that hath meat, let him do likewise" Luke 3:10-11 (KJV).

Later, Jesus himself offered similar teachings when he said, "And unto him that smiteth thee on the one cheek offer also the other; and him that taketh away thy cloke forbid not to take thy coat also. Give to every man that asketh of thee; and of him that taketh away thy goods ask them not again. And as ye would that men should do to you, do ye also to them likewise" Luke 6:29-31 (KJV).

These teachings do tend to transcend just doing unto others, but they are instructions concerning dealing with other people none the less and thus need to be seriously considered.

A little down to earth fiction is an example for teaching people to do unto others. In Aesop's Fables there is the story of The Lion and The Mouse and it goes something like this.

There was a lion which had finished a very good dinner and had gone to sleep near the entrance of its cave. He was pleasantly dreaming about food and things when there was a slight pull on his mane. Half asleep he reached up with his paw and caught a mouse. The lion wondered what this little thing: was doing in his mane and threatened to eat the mouse. However, the mouse begged him not to eat him. He asked to be spared saying that he did not know he was pulling on the mane of the lion. He thought rather it was a haystack where he could get hay for his nest. The mouse told the lion that he would repay him if he let him go. Well the lion was amused with the conceit of the mouse. He let him go because of his argument.

One day a hunting party out searching for lions for the royal zoo captured the lion. The hunters tied him up while they waited to transport him.

The mouse heard the roars of the lion. He thought he recognized them. He ran to the sight to see the lion desperately trying to break loose.

The mouse then ran up to the lion and assured him that he could set him free. He began to gnaw on the ropes until they were weak enough to be broken by the lion. When the lion was free the mouse said, "I told you I would repay you some day, now you can see. I have kept my word. Even a tiny mouse can help a lion."

Now, this little story is hardly reality, but it is reflective of reality. If we thought about it a few minutes most of us could probably come up with examples of times when we helped someone and that person came back at a later date and helped us when we were in need of help or just returned the favor by being nice. We consistently need someone around to be nice to us.

Enough of this section, we need only to say that one of the ways we need to live in order to make life more meaningful for ourselves is to do unto others as we would have them do for us. Not that we do for them so they will do for us, but that we do for them because we want to. Who knows, one day they may actually help us during our time of need. Or, perhaps they will help someone else.

Love Your Neighbor

Second, we must love our neighbor as ourselves. This point is too big for this chapter. Much has been written about it. However, I'll try to develop it briefly. It is too important to avoid for lack of space or time. I present it here also even though it is a rather ambiguous point to develop and even though love is an experience that is extremely hard to define.

In the teachings of Jesus we see that he said, "Ye have heard that it hath been said, Thou shalt love thy neighbour, and hate thine enemy. But I say unto you, Love your enemies, bless them that curse you, do good to them that hate you, and pray for them which despitefully use you, and persecute you; That ye may be the children of your Father which is in heaven: for he maketh his sun to rise on the evil and on the good, and sendeth rain on the just and on the unjust. For if ye love them which love you, what reward have ye? do not even the publicans the same? And if ye salute your brethren only, what do ye more than others? do not even the publicans so? Be ye therefore perfect, even as your Father which is in heaven is perfect" Matthew 5:43-48 (KJV).

Here is one of Jesus' illustrations of the understanding of the law. It is that portion of the law that is concerned with loving our neighbors. Jesus is trying to instruct us of the importance of loving our neighbors and goes on to say, "For if ye love them which love you, what reward have ye?"

Further teachings in scripture which exhort and encourage us to love our neighbor are numerous and found throughout the New Testament, but in Paul's first letter to the Corinthians we see what I feel is the most beautiful passage concerning love ever written. "Though I speak with the tongues of men and of angels, and have not charity, I am become as sounding brass, or a tinkling cymbal. [2] And though I have the gift of prophecy, and understand all mysteries, and all knowledge; and though I have all faith, so that I could remove mountains, and have not charity, I am nothing. [3] And though I bestow all my goods to feed the poor, and though I give my body to be burned, and have not charity, it profiteth me nothing. [4] Charity suffereth long, and is kind; charity envieth not; charity vaunteth not itself, is not puffed up, [5] Doth not behave itself unseemly, seeketh not her own, is not easily provoked, thinketh no evil; [6] Rejoiceth not in iniquity, but rejoiceth in the truth; [7] Beareth all things, believeth all things, hopeth all things, endureth all things. [8] Charity never faileth: but whether there be prophecies, they shall fail; whether there be tongues, they shall cease; whether there be knowledge, it shall vanish away.

1 Corinthians 13:1-8a (KJV).

Erich Fromm in his hook "The Art of Loving" points out the importance of love to us as individuals. His assertion in part is not about being loved, but about loving. Further, the issue is not only about being loved, but about being lovable. This position throws being loved into our laps. Being lovable is our responsibility. It is a means to being loved. "The deepest need of man, then, is the need to overcome his separateness, to leave the prison of his aloneness"

(p. 9). We need to have love in our lives in order to feel a part of existence and life. It is the only way we can overcome the separation we have from the creation and from community (family, friends, and society) of which we are a part but from which we now seem to be separate.

Therefore since we need love so much we need to love others as ourselves so we can gain a sense of closeness with our environment. By loving our neighbors as ourselves we set up a bridge of communication to others that we are loving persons. This makes it easier for them to love us. I wish the world maintained unconditional positive love or regard. This is rare. By being loveable we assume such personal stance by doing unto others as we would have them do unto us. In this we love others as we would have them love us and thus we have tied two ways of living together. We love ourselves and we love others. We can also say that loving others is a way to love ourselves with integrity rather than self-centeredness.

How do we live? We do unto others as we would have them do unto us. What is it we do? We love our neighbor as our self.

Love the Lord

This brings us to my finale point on how we should live.

We must love the Lord God with all our heart and mind and soul and strength, and again we turn to Jesus to see his words: "And one of the scribes came, and having heard them reasoning together, and perceiving that he had answered them well, asked him, Which is the first commandment of all? And Jesus answered him, The first of all the commandments is, Hear, O Israel; The Lord our God is one Lord: And thou shalt love the Lord thy God with all thy heart, and with all thy soul, and with all thy mind, and with all thy strength: this is the first commandment" Mark 12:28-30 (KJV).

However, in this day and age, how do we come to love God as we should?

We come to love God because he first loved us and sent his son into the world. Let me refer to John's first letter: "Beloved, let us love one another: for love is of God; and every one that loveth is born of God, and knoweth God. He that not loveth not knoweth God; for God is love. In this was manifested the love of God toward us, because that God sent his only begotten Son into the world, that we might live through him. Herein is love, not that we loved God, but that he loved us, and sent his Son to be the propitiation for our sins. Beloved, if God so loved us, we ought also to love one another. No man hath seen God at any time. If we love one another, God dwelleth in us, and his love is perfected in us. Hereby know we that we dwell in him, and he in us, because he hath given us of his Spirit" 1 John 4:7-13 (KJV).

In this we see that we can love God because he loved us. Also because he loved us we can love others. So we can again ask.

How do we live? We do unto others as we would have them do unto us.

What do we do unto others? We love our neighbors as ourselves.

How are we able to love our neighbors as ourselves? We are able to do this because we love God with all our heart and mind and soul and strength.

Then how are we able to love God as we should? We are able to love God because he first loved us and manifested his love in us by sending his Son into the world to be the expiation for our sins and "because he hath given us of his Spirit" 1 John 4:13 (KJV).

References

Fromm, E. (1956). The art of loving. New York, NY: Perennial Classics – HarperCollins Publishers.

God Forgives Our Denial

After all this reflection of faith, getting it, having it, and benefitting from it, there is an issue of denial. Walking outside the realm of faith, a person has been in denial that Jesus is the Christ. Even when people have faith, denial of Jesus is not uncommon. This denial has to be overcome. It is forgiven in relationship to God's grace.

In recognizing that God forgives denial, there are some presuppositions that need to be kept in mind as this chapter unfolds. These include the idea that denial is a symptom of sin. Sin is that destructive force within us all that leads to our ultimate death. It leads us to do wrong. Sin defies psychological, sociological, cultural, and physical explanation.

It is to sin that Christ died. Christ's death enabled God to forgive us of our sins, our wrong doings, in this case the sin of denial. Since Christ died to sin and since we join with him in that death, we hope to realize that God forgives our sins, even though we are still in sin and are sinners. We also hope to realize that even if we deny our Lord Jesus Christ from time to time, He will not reject us if we have faith in him.

Picture, if you will a courtyard. There is a courtyard laid out in the center of a two or three story building in or near Jerusalem. The walls may be sandy colored or tan. There are plants located in various places about the courtyard. It is night time and the stars are shining and twinkling. The moon is glowing just over the top of the building itself. There is a slight breeze that is gently blowing around the courtyard.

Over in the corner, away from the entrance gate, is a fairly large fire. There are people clustered around the fire. Others are roaming about the courtyard. It is by the fire that we see Peter. He had followed the crowd of people that played a part in the capture of Jesus. The crowd is mainly made up of guards and some bystanders. Much jabbering is taking place. Peter though is not participating in it. There is a certain tension and anxiety in the air. Peter is somewhat withdrawn and protective in this environment. He is warming his hands over the fire. His elbows in close and shoulders shrugged. As we look at his head, it is bent forward. He is looking at his hands. He is chilly. He is angry. He is angry. He is curious. And, he is scared.

A woman who is dressed like a maid or servant of the high priest approaches Peter. She addresses him, apparently recognizing something about him.

"Aren't you with Jesus?" she asks.

"No," Peter curtly responds and moves away from the fire.

As the maid mingles in the crowd, she approaches other bystanders about Peter's affiliation with Jesus.

"Surely, this man is with Jesus," she says to them.

Peter over hears this and all but yells. "I don't know the man." He denies again he knows Jesus.

He moves into the gateway. However, he is approached by a bystander who wants to make sure Peter is not one of Christ's followers.

"You are with him!" the bystander says emphatically.

"Man, I don't know him!" Peter shouts.

Suddenly, a rooster crows. Peter remembers what Christ had told him at the supper the evening before the event.

Peter breaks down and wails. With his tears, he can hardly see.

This is Peter, the rock. One of our Biblical heroes denied Christ. He has sinned against Christ and against God. Can it be that Peter was human, a mere sinner. Yes! And Peter is forgiven for that wrong doing. The Christ he denied is the Christ who died on the cross for the forgiveness of sins. The Christ who died on the cross is the Christ who was raised from the dead. "God raised Him up again, putting an end to the agony of death, since it was impossible for Him to be held in its power" Acts 2:24 (NASB). The very Christ that Peter denied is the Christ Peter proclaimed in faith.

Now visualize if you can a lone corridor in a hospital. There are the typical wells with the tile halfway to the top. Large doorways are seen at intervals along the hall. To the right, the hall ends at a door which leads to another wing of the hospital. To the left, is the way to the elevators. In front of you is drinking fountain. Two young men are beside it. One is a little hefty and blond headed, about 5'10." The other is dark haired and just a little bit smaller in height. The two are talking to each other. OK, the dark haired young man is me.

Bob: "Doug, you ought to go into the ministry."

Doug: "You have got to be kidding. I don't want to be any part of that race."

Bob: "But your life style is so similar to that of a minister and it fits your beliefs."

Doug: "Listen, I don't have any intention of going along with the junk that a minister has to do."

It is real easy to see I didn't have a great deal of respect for the profession of minister at the time.

Now, you are in a recovery room. It has nine oxygen units and accompanying these are suction units. There are yellow drapes used for dividers. A patient has arrived and I am at the desk putting a couple of things into a briefcase. The doctor, dressed in a grayish green scrub suit is taking a seat at the desk as I moved toward the patient. The doctor asks what I have been studying. "Some history," I responded.

What I really was studying was American religious history for seminary. I did not own up to what I was doing watering down the topic to make it safer. I feel it was a mild way of denying Jesus is the Christ. I did not fess up to what I was doing. "I neither know nor understand what you mean" might as well have been said. In short, I experienced fear and the possibility of being associated with Christ. The situation was hardly as intense as the situation in which Peter found himself, but it was still a form of denial.

So, where does this leave me? Am I rejected for denying Christ?

No sir! No more so than Peter was rejected. I am still a Christian. I am forgiven for my denial, my sin, delivered and freed from sin through Christ.

Here's another scene. It is a living room. A sofa which is early Salvation Army, the paintings on the wall are from a well-known, but middle-class, store. They were obtained during one of those half-off sales. The plush carpet has some bleach spots where the sunlight shines through the window. A gorgeous stereo was inherited from a grandparent after she got a new one.

Tonight a friend is coming over. Someone you met at a local music store. You both expressed an interest in the same new album. So you invited this person over to listen to that album. There is of course a certain anxiety and tension about whether or not you will be accepted as a person to his new friend.

It is now 7:30 P.M. and you are making final preparations, clearing the coffee table.

Your guest is knocking at the door. Hurriedly you place the Bible on an end table and proceed to answer the door. In the process of doing so, you forget about the Bible.

During the course of the evening at your humble abode, you have gotten the record started. Then about halfway thru the record as the conversation progresses, your visitor expresses some hostility towards Christianity. A certain tension develops, for you, and at that very moment, you have spotted your Bible on the table. Somehow you carry on your conversation by reflecting on what was said by your visitor. You get up and start to take your Bible to another room. But your visitor asks you about the book you are carrying out of the living room. You respond by saying that it is a Bible, one of your relatives left on the end table.

You have denied Christ. There is your Bible. It is not a relative's. You have sinned if you will. Yet, here you are stuck in your denial of Christ. Are you rejected by God for that act? By no means, for Christ Himself lifts you up from your inadequacies. After all, you may have been afraid or angry when you denied him. You were at least under the influence of sin. However, because of Christ and your faith in him, you are forgiven.

There are certainly more dangerous scenarios that Christians have encountered through the centuries. These expressed pale in comparison. With all that can be said, one can easily say that Christ has been denied in the past. Peter denied him. I have denied him and others have denied him in some way. Whether the denial is in the face of severe adversity, or in the safety of one's own living, denial that Jesus is the Christ or knowing him is a reality. There are no doubt psychological reasons for these denials. Certainly there are sociological forces at work. There are theological implications of sin, among them is the alienation that a sinner experiences. However, we have been relieved of the burden of sin by our Lord Jesus Christ.

Since we are sinners and since we have denied Christ in the past is absolutely no reason to think we will not deny Him again. Indeed, we will deny Him again. We are under the influence of sin even as grace and forgiveness is part of our experience in Christ. Even though sin no longer has dominion over us, because of Christ, and we are forgiven of our denial, we will continue to sin. God will continue to forgive us.

No one can then say we will not deny him, not do wrong, or not sin if we accept what He has done for us. For sin is still a reality. It just does not have the power to destroy us, because Christ defeated sin's "sting of death" Christ redeemed us through forgiveness. God forgives our denials, our sins.

A Study Of James - Part 1

"My brethren, count it all joy when ye fall into divers temptations; Knowing this, that the trying of your faith worketh patience. But let patience have her perfect work, that ye may be perfect and entire, wanting nothing" James 1:2-4 (KJV)

"Count it all joy" in the midst of different trials? Talk about something impossible, this is impossible. At least it seems so. It appears to be asking a great deal. How can we expect to be joyful over trials and tribulations? It is almost masochistic, "more pain, I love it, just lay it on me." Can you see us in that role? Why should we be there? We would be crazy to walk such a road of having pain inflicted on us so we can experience joy. That's a little perverted, don't you think? Fortunately, that isn't what James is indicating here.

We are charged to be joyful, because testing produces steadfastness. Maybe here we can strike a little closer to home with all of us. Each of us has had a traumatic experience in our lives and experienced extreme pain during its duration. Perhaps we have lost a valuable friend or relative. Perhaps we see someone we care about caught up in drugs, alcohol, crime, or tribulation. So, we experience pain.

I don't think James is trying to say, don't have any pain. Rather in relationship to pain, also be joyful in anticipation. The joy comes from anticipation of a better state of mind which is experienced during tribulation through faith. So, in this way we can walk hand in hand with the Biblical teaching "grieve not, as those who have no hope." For those of us who have walked through storms and kept our eyes and hearts directed toward the Lord, even though we may have doubted His existence during this period, we became stronger in our faith. Thus, we also became more steadfast in our faith. And this makes it possible to experience joy while suffering, but not as the result of suffering, but as the result of hoping and realizing that we will become stronger at the end of each trial.

It may be asked what we should do with pain, suffering, tribulation, and death. I suggest that part of the handling is the anticipation of deliverance coming with Christ's return. Well, James shows us that in the meantime, hope can be found in faith that is tested by trials.

The steadfastness has its effect in our lives by bringing us to perfection and completion. Here we find an answer to the problem of Christian perfection with which Wesley worked and with which many today are wrestling. There are groups today which are trying to be perfect by trying to purge Sin from their lives and thus become sinless. I remember seeing a television evangelist say he was sinless. I immediately switched channels. John Calvin pointed out, we are always sinners and need God's Grace daily. So perfection then does not come in this life with the alienation of Sin from our lives. I find it worth considering that steadfastness in faith in Jesus Christ is perfection: at least for now.

"If any of you lack wisdom, let him ask of God, that giveth to all men liberally, and upbraideth not; and it shall be given him. But let him ask in faith, nothing wavering. For he that wavereth is like a wave of the sea driven with the wind and tossed" James 1:5-6 (KJV).

If any lacks wisdom it will be given to those who ask for it. Here we find those verses used by many to say "if there is anything you need from God ask for it." Yet many of us have asked for things and have not received these things. Many arguments are presented to us concerning why this is so and one of these comes from this group of passages.

Let the person ask in faith with no doubt. Here we find the verse for the argument "if you only have enough faith when you ask then you'll get that for which you have asked." How many times have we heard this? How many times following prayer for something substantial such as the healing of a sick loved one when no healing took place did we feel guilty because we thought that we did not have enough faith? How many times have we been disappointed and disillusioned with God because of these presuppositions? James does not offer help here. "For let not that man think that he shall receive any thing of the Lord" James 1:7 (KJV). Doubt is seen as the obstacle.

More guilt plus inferiority can be had for us in the interpretations of verse 8. "A double minded man is unstable in all his ways" James 1:8 (KJV). This unstable person in all his ways should not suppose he would have prayers answered. So when our prayers are not answered we feel we must be unstable for the scriptures say we are. The Greek word (akatastatos) is not a psychological word, at least not in sense of psychopathology. This is not about mental illness for instance. It is about inconsistency. It is about losing focus.

Unfortunately for us, the suppositions are true. We do ask with doubt in our hearts and we do ask while being unstable (inconsistent) in all our ways. After all, these are why we need a savior and why God came Himself into this world to save us. So, since these are true we must take the blame for our condition.

However, we must also hope that though we are in this predicament, we are going to be delivered and changed into faithful and stable persons when our Lord and Savior Jesus Christ returns. In the meantime, sometimes we will get a taste of what it will be like through the faith that we do have now.

"Let the brother of low degree rejoice in that he is exalted: But the rich, in that he is made low: because as the flower of the grass he shall pass away. For the sun is no sooner risen with a burning heat, but it withereth the grass, and the flower thereof falleth, and the grace of the fashion of it perisheth: so also shall the rich man fade away in his ways" James 1:9-11 (KJV)

This section is an indication of one very significant ideal. That in Christ, the lowly are lifted up and the rich are humbled. It certainly is consistent with the parable of Lazarus and the rich man of Luke 16:19-31. James' twist is that he points out that all are equal in the eyes of the Lord God almighty. There is really no difference in our lives because we are all sinners. So Christ shows the lowly they are worthy of His love despite their inferiority complex and He shows the rich how much they need Him despite their self-centeredness and self love.

"Blessed is the man that endureth temptation: for when he is tried, he shall receive the crown of life, which the Lord hath promised to them that love him. Let no man say when he is tempted, I am tempted of God: for God cannot be tempted with evil, neither tempteth he any man: But every man is tempted, when he is drawn away of his own lust, and enticed. Then when lust hath conceived, it bringeth forth sin: and sin, when it is finished, bringeth forth death" James 1:12-15 (KJV).

Peirazo (the Greek) is about examination. The King James uses the word temptation which is often associated with enticement towards sin. The one who endures the examination will receive the crown of life as promised by God. How hard it is to hope in Christ during temptation and trial. For it is during these times in our lives that we have the most anger at God and the most doubt about God. Fortunately, we have the Holy Spirit to enlighten us concerning God and give us hope during our temptation that we will make it. For those who can hang on during trial and temptation the reward will be great and wonderful, "the crown of life."

Let no one say this temptation is from God. God is not the source of our trials and temptations. He makes no effort to do this to anyone. However, he does allow it to happen in our lives, but not without a comforter, if we accept it, namely the Holy Spirit. So if temptation comes not from God, from where does it come?

Each person is tempted from within. Temptation arises from inner desire. Our own urges and wants give rise to temptation. The very theological equivalent to Freud's Id concept lies here. The basic unsatisfiable drives, "give me, give me, give me" rest here. The Id takes all it can get and then keeps demanding more. If it weren't for the super-ego and ego, it would be interesting to see where we would be. I suspect, totally unable to resist temptation at all, certainly incapable of recognizing it.

When we give into our desires, this causes sin and sin leads to death. Now we need to be careful here for this explanation of sin does not go very deep. It deals more with the practical side of sin namely giving into our lusts, our greed, our anxieties, and/or our selfishness. These lead to sins with a little "s", but Sin is our total corruption, depravity, and alienation and this is the full grown Sin which leads to death.

"Do not err, my beloved brethren. Every good gift and every perfect gift is from above, and cometh down from the Father of lights, with whom is no variableness, neither shadow of turning. Of his own will begat he us with the word of truth, that we should be a kind of firstfruits of his creatures" James 1:16-18 (KJV).

In essence, to not be mistaken, for all which is good comes from God. There are those in the world who feel the things which are good for us; a good home, success, talents, fine family, etc., are the result of human efforts. A common myth is that some people think "money can buy happiness." If this were true, there would be easy formulas for all to follow which would lead people to all the good treasures in life. It could be obtained by having the right amount of money.

However, James asserts that God is the giver of gifts and not ourselves. If there is a formula for good gifts, it is to look for those gifts we have and not the ones we don't. The basis would be to look at the source of good gifts, God. This is not to say we should not try to better our lives, for to better our lives may lead us to another gift from God.

One of the good gifts He has given us is "the word of truth." The reason for this gift is so the world can see there is fruit to partake. So the Christian in witness to the word of truth is an example of the living word not through deeds but through hope in Jesus Christ which leads to deeds. The fruit of life is seen in the response of people to the Good News of the work of salvation. We know that Jesus Christ is given to the world so "that we should be a kind of firstfruits of his creatures." We are in this, made different and act differently.

"Wherefore, my beloved brethren, let every man be swift to hear, slow to speak, slow to wrath: For the wrath of man worketh not the righteousness of God. Wherefore lay apart all filthiness and superfluity of naughtiness, and receive with meekness the engrafted word, which is able to save your souls. But be ye doers of the word, and not hearers only, deceiving your own selves. For if any be a hearer of the word, and not a doer, he is like unto a man beholding his natural face in a glass: For he beholdeth himself, and goeth his way, and straightway forgetteth what manner of man he was. But whoso looketh into the perfect law of liberty, and continueth therein, he being not a forgetful hearer, but a doer of the work, this man shall be blessed in his deed. If any man among you seem to be religious, and bridleth not his tongue, but deceiveth his own heart, this man's religion is vain. Pure religion and undefiled before God and the Father is this, To visit the fatherless and widows in their affliction, and to keep himself unspotted from the world" James 1:19-27 (KJV).

I would suspect those struggling with keeping James in Bible the formative years of the saved by grace not by works theology found this problematic. There are works here.

I assert the works described here though are faith. That does not mean we will carry them out because we have faith. However, we can't carry them out without faith.

"Let every man be swift to hear, slow to speak, slow to wrath"" For all of us, this is difficult. We seem to find it hard to live up to these expectations. Some have more trouble with it than others. They live up to the statement "open mouth, insert foot" all too often and regret it.

Yet, there is a practical side to these instructions. It can keep us from embarrassing ourselves. It helps us make sure we know what we are talking about if we take the time to evaluate what we are reacting to.

"The wrath of man worketh not the righteousness of God." This is not to put down the value of anger. It is important to get angry just as Jesus did at the temple. However, it is important to realize that our anger does not do the work of God. God does His own work and presents His own righteousness. We can't do that on our own.

So, let us "put away" our filthiness and wickedness and receive the word which is able to do the work we cannot do. This is why we need to do what we can in order to follow God's instructions. These instructions are designed to let God work righteousness for us. They are not designed to make us better on our own merit. They deliver us from evil and wickedness and Sin on the strength of God's authority and will.

Therefore, "be ye doers of the word, and not hearers only." If we want life in Christ to be more real to us then we must follow God's instructions the best we can. This is not the legalism of the commandments, but the evidence of God's holy presence in our lives. "But this shall be the covenant that I will make with the house of Israel; After those days, saith the LORD, I will put my law in their inward parts, and write it in their hearts; and will be their God, and they shall be my people. And they shall teach no more every man his neighbour, and every man his brother, saying, Know the LORD: for they shall all know me, from the least of them unto the greatest of them, saith the LORD: for I will forgive their iniquity, and I will remember their sin no more" Jeremiah 31:33-34 (KJV). Otherwise it will be as if we never met God in the first place and our trials and tribulations will be all the more frustrating for there will be a lower hope in Christ which will make it more difficult for us. However, the one who looks *"into the perfect law of liberty, and continueth therein, he being not a forgetful hearer, but a doer of the work, this man shall be blessed in his deed."* Dare we see the willingness to be "a doer of the work" as the blessing? Rather, than legalism, this is grace and mercy. God helps us act differently.

"If any man among you seems to be religious, and bridleth not his tongue . . . this man's religion is vain." This does not stand alone. It essentially echoes being "slow to speak." Charges from nonbelievers that we are hypocrites may hinge on whether we keep this aspect of the faith or not. Hereto, this needs to be an indicator or our focus on and openness to God and His presence. If we pop off our mouths and hurt others with disparaging remarks, or gossip about someone, we may not have a direct impact on them, but we do have an impact on perceptions of our faith. Are we willing to practice what we preach?

True religion finds its reality in such things as visiting "the fatherless and widows in their affliction, and to keep himself unspotted from the world." There is nothing here that says we will always live up to this. It certainly puts us in a position to observe that no one does always live up to this. There are other charges and commandments. Still, it is a good indicator of our faith.

A Study Of James - Part 2

"My brethren, have not the faith of our Lord Jesus Christ, the Lord of glory, with respect of persons. For if there come unto your assembly a man with a gold ring, in goodly apparel, and there come in also a poor man in vile raiment; And ye have respect to him that weareth the gay clothing, and say unto him, Sit thou here in a good place; and say to the poor, Stand thou there, or sit here under my footstool: Are ye not then partial in yourselves, and are become judges of evil thoughts? Hearken, my beloved brethren, Hath not God chosen the poor of this world rich in faith, and heirs of the kingdom which he hath promised to them that love him? But ye have despised the poor. Do not rich men oppress you, and draw you before the judgment seats? Do not they blaspheme that worthy name by which ye are called?" James 2:1-7 (KJV)

The Revised Standard Version begins the chapter saying, "Show no partiality as you hold the faith of our Lord Jesus Christ . . . ." James here is thus noting that we do indeed show partiality even though he has just told us that we are not to show partiality. It is a fact of life that we do make distinctions in the status of people. We continually lift up certain of our people onto a pedestal for viewing.

There are several prime examples of this. One of these is the rich. We continually place these people in another category. It seems that those who are able to accumulate great wealth have been given a special status in life and have taken full advantage of it. Whatever the rich person wants, it seems the rich person gets.

A person of great wealth who was widely recognized in the world was Nelson Rockefeller. This man amassed millions of dollars in property, stocks, bonds, and other investments. He was a part of the politics of the country for many years. You can bet your life that if he walked into a Church he would have received a very warm reception. He would have been given the very best of attention that we or any other person could give. He probably would have been invited to say a word or two to the congregation. After the service he would probably have been invited to lunch with someone from the congregation. Of course, it would only be with the person or persons of the highest status with whom he would have sat down to eat. I mean, that is the way I image it would probably be. After all, life is like that and partiality is shown.

Another example of high status and high partiality is that of the physician. Here are men and women who have trained many, many years to learn medical health care. When they set up practice they take care of a lot of people. But it is interesting that many of the people who go into medicine do not go into it to help people, rather they go into it for its financial security. It is a financial security which is made possible by the people, who are cared for. We, as people, tend to lift up physicians almost to the level of gods. They are expected to know all, heal all, and cure all. These people get special discounts, free gifts, and many fringe benefits in life for the role they play in society.

Another example of people holding high partiality is athletes. When a person is willing to pay another person millions of dollars just to throw and hit a baseball, it is certain that such a person is being held in very high esteem. That does not mean the athlete is liked. A specific example of an athlete being held in high esteem was Fran Tarkenton. Here was a man who leads all quarterbacks in the history of football in many categories. He was for a time the premiere record holder in the NFL today. And because of his accomplishments, he has been reaping the harvest of benefits for years and believe me it has been a harvest. He presently is a successful businessman. The best I can tell, Fran Tarkenton has had a good reputation contrary to other superstars who were arrogant and problematic.

I could continue to give examples, but already I have been entirely too redundant and repetitious in this area concerning our showing partiality. There is an interesting psychological interpretation for our showing partiality to people which I would like to share with you.

In the 1974 Pulitzer Prize winning book "Denial of Death" written by the late Earnest Becker, there is seen a very interesting explanation for our showing partiality. Becker labels this hero worship. Basically what Becker says is this, all of us in order to eliminate the reality of death from our lives, gear our lives in such a way to accomplish this. One of the ways we do this is through having heroes. By placing people in a special category and placing them in a position of idols, we essentially try to make them immortal and thus make them god. In so doing, we distract ourselves from the reality that we all are mortal. We thus suppress or sublimate our fears of death. Now, this is just one of the ways we deny death and we will not get into that subject here, but I wanted you to see why we are subject to partiality in people.

"Hath not God chosen the poor of this world rich in faith?" We have to be careful with our partiality for it does not really accomplish anything anyhow. We become no better for making heroes of others. Those we look at to be our heroes aren't any different than we are anyway. On top of that, when we really think about the persons who have had the most profound inspiration for us, they tend to be people who lead rather simple lives. One of those was my 6th grade teacher, Mr. Ritz. In helping people who are homeless, unemployed, and who had difficulty getting enough to eat, I have often been inspired by their faith. I have met rich people who were not as thankful as some of the poor people I have met.

"If ye fulfil the royal law according to the scripture, Thou shalt love thy neighbour as thyself, ye do well: But if ye have respect to persons, ye commit sin, and are convinced of the law as transgressors. For whosoever shall keep the whole law, and yet offend in one point, he is guilty of all. For he that said, do not commit adultery, said also, do not kill. Now if thou commit no adultery, yet if thou kill, thou art become a transgressor of the law. So speak ye, and so do, as they that shall be judged by the law of liberty. For he shall have judgment without mercy, that hath shewed no mercy; and mercy rejoiceth against judgment" James 2:8-13 (KJV).

For anyone who fails in one point concerning the law is guilty of transgressing the whole law. Here James endeavors to make things hard for us and tries to show us that in order to fulfill the law we have to live up to all the law. We cannot break one of the laws without breaking the whole law. We must love our neighbors as ourselves. We must also not commit adultery. We must not kill. There are many other aspects of the law which we have to follow. The point doesn't become more difficult than that.

Yet, I said James was making it difficult for us. He actually was pointing to our imperfection. In fact, in spite of the admonitions to practice the faith, these are made because believers are still sinners who fail to keep the law. The realization of this helps us not to be focused on the law and become dependent on it, but upon grace and mercy.

"So speak ye, and so do, as they that shall be judged by the law of liberty." If we are to fulfill the law, then we need to speak and act accordingly. This is not about just adhering to the law which we fail to do anyway, but to depend on God to carry the day. For judgment will come by the law. It will take into consideration whether or not we live up to every aspect of the law. It will not be favorable to us for living up to parts of the law at the neglect of other parts. We will be judged only by whether or not we are doing what God wants us to do, namely, fulfilling the law through faith and allowing God to overcome our short-comings. "For he shall have judgment without mercy, that hath shewed no mercy; and mercy rejoiceth against judgment." If we break the law we deserve whatever judgment is handed to us. If we show no mercy, we won't receive mercy. So in the example of our showing partiality towards some, at the neglect of others, we break the law. In breaking the law, we are thus subject to the judgment which comes with breaking the law. All of us have broken the law in some form or another and are thus subject to judgment. So where does relief for our judgment come?

The English Standard Version reads, "Mercy triumphs over judgment." My take on this also is that by walking in the mercy of God and acting accordingly, we escape judgment. For this could very well mean that only God's mercy will overcome judgment. Only God's judgment can determine whether or not we have lived up to the law of God and walk in mercy. Since we have not lived up to the law and as the scriptures say, "all have fallen short of the glory of God," and even our "righteousness is as filthy rags," we need God's mercy through Jesus Christ which is, to my understanding, totally capable of triumphing and winning out over judgment.

"What doth it profit, my brethren, though a man say he hath faith, and have not works? can faith save him? [15] If a brother or sister be naked, and destitute of daily food, [16] And one of you say unto them, Depart in peace, be ye warmed and filled; notwithstanding ye give them not those things which are needful to the body; what doth it profit? [17] Even so faith, if it hath not works, is dead, being alone. [18] Yea, a man may say, Thou hast faith, and I have works: shew me thy faith without thy works, and I will shew thee my faith by my works" James 2:14-18 (KJV)

James confronts an important issue regarding faith and works. Essentially it can be stated, somebody can say, "You hold faith and I hold works. Let me see your faith without works, and I will show by works my faith. Faith enables works. These works are not my works or my efforts. They are not the works of the believer, or the believer's efforts. The believer does consciously participate in these works. Paul's often used verse, "For by grace are ye saved through faith; and that not of yourselves: it is the gift of God: Not of works, lest any man should boast" Ephesians 2:8-9 (KJV) almost always go uncompleted.

Taken out of the context to illustrate the saved by faith, not by works position, the following passage gets left out. This is a statement, even a definition of faith: "For we are his workmanship, created in Christ Jesus unto good works, which God hath before ordained that we should walk in them" Ephesians 2:10 (KJV). It defines what true faith is.

"Thou believest that there is one God; thou doest well: the devils also believe, and tremble. But wilt thou know, O vain man, that faith without works is dead? Was not Abraham our father justified by works, when he had offered Isaac his son upon the altar? Seest thou how faith wrought with his works, and by works was faith made perfect? And the scripture was fulfilled which saith, Abraham believed God, and it was imputed unto him for righteousness: and he was called the Friend of God. Ye see then how that by works a man is justified, and not by faith only. Likewise also was not Rahab the harlot justified by works, when she had received the messengers, and had sent them out another way? For as the body without the spirit is dead, so faith without works is dead also" James 2:19-26 (KJV)

This is a great point. Faith does not simply believe that Jesus died on the cross for the forgiveness of sins. James points out that even the demons know that. It does them no good as they remain standing in rebellion and resistance to God's grace, mercy, love, and forgiveness. Here we have the verses of scripture which throw the biggest bone into the works of protestant theology especially Lutheran theology. Luther, in his study of Romans, came to grasp the idea of salvation by Faith alone. He recognized that only through Faith could one be saved, and of course, the Faith was in Jesus Christ.

Mainline protestant thinking has inherited this thinking. Many theologians over the years have proclaimed the principle. From Luther to Calvin to Wesley until this very day, it was and is accepted that in order to be saved, one is saved through Faith in Jesus Christ. Works are not capable of bringing us into justification before God. Only Faith can work our redemption and justification and sanctification for us.

James presents the neglected aspect of faith. Paul did too. It just is ignored, or rejected. However, James, in the verses presented above, causes us some serious problems concerning works and faith. "What doth it profit, my brethren, though a man say he hath faith, and have not works? can faith save him?" These are very legitimate questions. And the answer to the questions include: how can a believer have faith and no works? How can a believer even be a believer without having works? If we turn to the words of our Lord as seen in the book of John, we see the words "If ye love me, keep my commandments" John 14:15 (KJV). That is faith.

Further, coming to the realization that God loved us enough to send his son into the world to save us is the essence of faith and thus coming to an understanding of that compassion, surely is so powerful to over flow in us. However, the second part of James' question, "can faith save him?" is harder to answer. For how can sinners be expected to do good works? Even the scriptures recognize the problem of Sin and that no good thing is in our hearts. So on this ground alone, faith at times is all we have for we know we sin even as believers. We would therefore have to say yes, a person's faith without works can save him. It may be all we have.

Based on these presuppositions the following verse may or may not be agreeable to us. "So faith without works is dead also." As already mentioned, if we confront the love of God in Jesus Christ and if it is indeed powerful enough to save us from our sins, then surely this will influence our lives and radiate out toward the world. Yet, as sinners are we capable of conveying love and only capable of listening to the desires of the flesh as Paul said, "For we know that the law is spiritual: but I am carnal, sold under sin . . . For I know that in me (that is, in my flesh,) dwelleth no good thing: for to will is present with me; but how to perform that which is good I find not"

Romans 7:14&18 (KJV). So, if we are incapable of works then it means salvation through faith is the only alternative.

Repeating, "Yea, a man may say, Thou hast faith, and I have works: shew me thy faith without thy works, and I will shew thee my faith by my works." There is no advance on this argument. There is no way I can prove my faith without demonstrating it through works which is love from God as faith is love from God. Yet this verse also lends itself to self-righteousness. "See, I am closer to eternal life than you are for you can see my works."

What a tension. Faith is about Jesus as Savior. It is about discovering God forgives us for being sinners. James says Faith is about works, holy works wrought be God in our lives. To simply believe that Jesus is the Christ is not enough. Works that are of God in our lives, make Faith what it is. Works cannot really be separated from Faith. The works of Faith can be distinguished from our works. The works of faith though are not the works of sinners. They are the works of God in believers.

A Study Of James - Part 3

"My brethren, be not many masters, knowing that we shall receive the greater condemnation. For in many things we offend all. If any man offend not in word, the same is a perfect man, and able also to bridle the whole body" James 3:1-2 (KJV).

"My brethren, be not many masters, knowing that we shall receive the greater condemnation." Modern translations use the word "teacher" instead of "master." Do not let this statement about "condemnation" keep you from teaching about the Word of God. For we have to have teachers. Besides, this is not concerned with ability. It is concerned with correct teachings. It states that judgment is stricter concerning teachers because they are responsible for passing on the truth of God's teachings to others. Any perversion of the Gospel of Our Lord is subject to judgment. So, do not be concerned with ability, but with the accuracy of teaching which is confirmed by scripture and tradition and the witness of the Holy Spirit.

The Revised Standard Version translates James 3:2, "For we all make many mistakes, and if anyone makes no mistakes in what he says, he is a perfect man." With all the differing interpretations of Scripture that exist, all of us probably have failed to understand. That is what grace is for. We have to trust that God will forgive us for our errors in understanding. So teach with humility.

Since, we all make mistakes; we need to expect to be wrong concerning our conclusions about the teachings of the Word. Thus, it must be that God will take this into consideration during our judgment. We are subject to sin, and thus make mistakes and errors. Strict judgment will fall on those who deliberately and purposefully reject the concepts of scripture. Those who deliberately contradict God's word will encounter strict judgment. It will fall on those who pervert the Gospel and teach perversion as truth.

The possibility of error in relationship to this need not be frightening to us. We are subject to mistakes and this is verified in Wesley's teachings concerning Christian perfection. Further, it can also be seen in the teachings of John Calvin, who also wrote about error and mistakes made on the part of believers. For we do not have all the answers and do not know all there is to know, thus we are subject to misinterpretation.

Some prime examples concerning mistakes include: predestination, eternal life, and perfection. In the area of predestination, we hear the argument from the Calvinistic school which states that God has chosen some people for salvation even though they deserve eternal punishment. For some in this school, God, it is said, has chosen to damn the rest for they too deserve eternal punishment. There are several scriptural references which talk about the chosen people of God and the predestined under God: Jeremiah 1:5; Jude 1:4; Galatians 1:15, among others.

However, the other side of the argument represented by Wesley and the Arminians also has scriptural support. This argument says that the human being, even though he is lost and defiled before God, still has something of the divine spark in him. When confronted by the Holy Spirit there is an interaction which can, if the human being wills and chooses to respond, witness with his spirit to show him he is a child of God. Salvation then comes to those who choose to respond rather than to just a select whom God chooses to save, for God chooses to save everyone. Election then comes when one accepts God's gift of salvation. Surely, if man was created in the Image of God, something of what that means remains.

Another area subject to mistake is the area concerning eternal life. There is a large emphasis being placed on what happens to us when we die and our body dies. Some assert that our soul goes to heaven. One Biblical incident indicating this is related to Jesus' death on the cross. "And one of the malefactors which were hanged railed on him, saying, If thou be Christ, save thyself and us. But the other answering rebuked him, saying, Dost not thou fear God, seeing thou art in the same condemnation? And we indeed justly; for we receive the due reward of our deeds: but this man hath done nothing amiss. And he said unto Jesus, Lord, remember me when thou comest into thy kingdom. And Jesus said unto him, Verily I say unto thee, To day shalt thou be with me in paradise" Luke 23:39-43 (KJV). I am hard pressed to find a great deal of support for further passages supporting this position. There is little scriptural evidence for this and that which does support it only implies a concept of heaven for us. The idea of the soul living on after death is foreign to Judeo-Christian teachings and comes from Greek thinking. This demonstrated by Leslie Stevenson (1987) in "Seven Theories of Human Nature." "It is a common and recurrent misinterpretation of Christian doctrine that it asserts a dualism between the material body and an immaterial soul or mind. Such dualism is a Greek idea and is not to be found in the Old or New Testaments. In the early centuries of the Church, Christian theology began to employ ideas of Greek philosophy in its formulations of doctrine, and the theology of immaterial soul did find its way into Christian thinking and has tended to stay there ever since" (p. 45).

The teaching concerning eternal life which has more Scriptural support is the resurrection from the dead. Scriptural support for this is numerous and thus many verses can be found which address it. It is based on the notion that the body, the soul, and the spirit are actually one and inseparable, and it means that when we die, we die totally. However, our fate rests in the hands of God and we will be dead until the resurrection comes with Christ's return. Thus Paul rightly considers the dead in Christ to be asleep until that time. "But I would not have you to be ignorant, brethren, concerning them which are asleep, that ye sorrow not, even as others which have no hope. For if we believe that Jesus died and rose again, even so them also which sleep in Jesus will God bring with him" 1 Thessalonians 4:13-14 (KJV).

The last area subject to mistake is that of Christian perfection. Here there is a mistake in that through Christ working in our lives we become perfect and follow the law of God to the letter. This ignores the fact that we are sinners in constant need of God's Grace and redemption. Perfection for now is in Christ, not in us. However, we will be made like him when we are raised from the dead.

I still remember being turned off by a television preacher who asserted he was sinless. I don't remember who he was. I am pretty sure it was not a well-known evangelist.

When I was ordained as a deacon in the North Georgia Conference of the United Methodist Church, we were asked, "Are you moving on to perfection?" We were expected to say, yes. I am now convinced that none of us knew what we were saying.

"Behold, we put bits in the horses' mouths, that they may obey us; and we turn about their whole body. Behold also the ships, which though they be so great, and are driven of fierce winds, yet are they turned about with a very small helm, whithersoever the governor listeth. Even so the tongue is a little member, and boasteth great things. Behold, how great a matter a little fire kindleth! And the

tongue is a fire, a world of iniquity: so is the tongue among our members, that it defileth the whole body, and setteth on fire the course of nature; and it is set on fire of hell. For every kind of beasts, and of birds, and of serpents, and of things in the sea, is tamed, and hath been tamed of mankind: But the tongue can no man tame; it is an unruly evil, full of deadly poison. Therewith bless we God, even the Father; and therewith curse we men, which are made after the similitude of God. Out of the same mouth proceedeth blessing and cursing. My brethren, these things ought not so to be. Doth a fountain send forth at the same place sweet water and bitter? Can the fig tree, my brethren, bear olive berries? either a vine, figs? so can no fountain both yield salt water and fresh" James 3:3-12 (KJV).

"And the tongue is a fire, a world of iniquity: so is the tongue among our members, that it defileth the whole body." This section of verses I believe can be seen as symbolic to our life, condition and predicament. I think it can be seen this way by three means. First, this look at the tongue can be compared with the fall of the world. Second, it can be seen as representing our goodness. Lastly, the tongue is also representative of our corruption.

First, this look by scripture at the tongue can be compared with the fall of the world. The tongue is seen as boasting of great things. As a fire, it is capable of causing destruction. Just as a small fire can set a forest ablaze, the tongue is able to stain the whole body. So here is the comparison. Just as the taking of the fruit from the tree of knowledge of good and evil brought corruption to Adam and Eve and to the world, and just as the sin of one man brought sin to all the world, the tongue has brought unrighteousness to the whole body for all to see. And in this way it is analogous to the Fall.

Second, the tongue can be seen as representing our goodness. With it, we can bless the Lord and Father. It is with the tongue that we form the very words which express love and praise for God and also love and praise for our fellow human beings. So it represents that part of us which is capable of expressing the fact that we were created in the image of God. So through the tongue we reflect the "Imago Dei".

Lastly, the tongue is also representative of our corruption. It can used to curse others, who are made in the image of God. It is with the tongue that we form the very words which express hate and hostility for God and also hate and hostility for our fellow human beings. So it represents that part of us which is defiled and corrupted and rebellious to God. It represents the fallen, sinful man. So through the tongue, we reflect the "sinner."

After a horrific shooting of Congresswoman Gabrielle Giffords in Tucson, Arizona on January 8, 2011, former Vice Presidential candidate Sara Palin came under fire for using the term "blood libel." Personally, I had never heard the use of the term that I can recall. However, the connotations were so negative as to cause of flurry of criticism. The term has been linked to anti-Semitic beliefs that Jews killed Christian babies as part of some religious rituals. One can see how that is offensive. It illustrates profoundly the impact of the tongue. What is said might have powerful negative consequences.

"Out of the same mouth proceedeth blessing and cursing. My brethren, these things ought not so to be so." The tongue then accurately is a symbol of our human situation. As the tongue blesses, we can be seen in the image of God, good and loving and kind. As the tongue curses, we can be seen as the fallen ones, evil and despising and rebellious.

The slant here is about being in control or at least advocates we should be in control. Since this ought not to be, it must be a reflection of our separation from God and in it we see our need for God to save and redeem us. Our tongue reflects our dilemma. We are creatures of God who have rebelled and who are in need of one to direct us back. We are the lost sheep who have wandered from the flock and we need the shepherd to come find us and take us back to the fold. Unfortunately, we are resisting the shepherd just like the sheep which is spirited and wanting to follow its curiosity and which is subject to harm by wolves and natural forces, we are spirited and wanting to follow our curiosity and are subject to harm by natural forces.

Yet, if the Holy Spirit works in us, and we are created in the image of God, surely we ought to be able to curb our tongues.

"Who is a wise man and endued with knowledge among you? let him shew out of a good conversation his works with meekness of wisdom. But if ye have bitter envying and strife in your hearts, glory not, and lie not against the truth. This wisdom descendeth not from above, but is earthly, sensual, devilish. For where envying and strife is, there is confusion and every evil work. But the wisdom that is from above is first pure, then peaceable, gentle, and easy to be intreated, full of mercy and good fruits, without partiality, and without hypocrisy. And the fruit of righteousness is sown in peace of them that make peace" James 3:13-18 (KJV)

"Who is a wise man and endued with knowledge among you? Let him shew out of a good conversation his works with meekness of wisdom." In these verses, we have some guidelines with which to determine how we should live. However, I am convinced that, since only a handful of people have lived up to these instructions, this may suggest God has set aside certain individuals to represent wisdom to this world. One of these characteristics of one who is wise and understanding is that he is able to show his works in the meekness of wisdom. Now this meekness is not the meekness of the world which is wishy-washy in nature being submissive and walking around with hands folded in front and speaking softly. Rather it is a meekness of God. One submits the self to God who is savior and redeemer. One gives up the idea that he is totally self-sufficient and takes on the idea that there is a God who is responsible for keeping all life going. No matter how smart, wise, loving, caring, hateful, mean, or deceptive a person is, or human kind is, God is the one behind all that exists and keeps things running. Evil can't prevail, and even goodness makes no contribution to the work of God.

"But if ye have bitter envying and strife in your hearts, glory not, and lie not against the truth." What this is saying is that if we have jealousy and ambition in our lives, we should not try to pretend we have the truth of God's wisdom in us. Unfortunately, a person who envies and does not glory God is prone to lying about God's truth or at least denying it. Further, we should not try to convince others we have the truth when we have jealousy and ambition, but that is precisely what we will do for sinners.

"This wisdom descendeth not from above, but is earthly, sensual, devilish." This verse demonstrates that jealousy and ambition does not come from God but is the result of the thinking of sinners. It therefore is recognized for what it is; earthly, unspiritual and devilish, the work of a sinful person who is incapable of recognizing the truth.

"For where envying and strife is, there is confusion and every evil work." It must be noted that the problem is expanding. Sin is no small thing and is not limited by one sin or two sins, but as we seriously look at Sin we see the investigation into its nature eventually leads us to realize there is a corruption that affects the whole world and not just individuals. It is an overwhelming, devastating reality and separates us from our Lord and master and creator.

"But the wisdom that is from above is first pure, then peaceable, gentle, and easy to be intreated, full of mercy and good fruits, without partiality, and without hypocrisy." Here I have to ask; do we see these things in anyone? And I have to say, "Yes." These qualities exist in many people, but not in an excess amount. For unfortunately all of us are sinners, jealous, ambitious, disorderly, and sinful. God has provided certain individuals with more wisdom than others, but even these people are still sinners.

So, where do we look for that wise person who represents the concept of wisdom seen here in James? Since we cannot even see it in ourselves, where do we turn? We see this person in Jesus Christ, only God himself could possibly walk this path, He, as a sinless man was capable of walking the road we should walk and ought to walk. But we cannot walk this road for we are sinners. So God had to walk it for us. In him, we find the wisdom, the purity, the peaceableness, the gentleness, the openness to reason, the fullness of mercy the good fruits, the certainty, and sincerity which we should have but don't. God is thus our righteousness and our wisdom. So it must be to him we turn to find our righteousness, for only he can do it for us, we cannot.

"And the fruit of righteousness is sown in peace of them that make peace." We need to accept Christ as our righteousness and wisdom to cover our mistakes regarding understanding and teaching. We have to assert that if this righteous Jesus is part of our lives, then we should be able, even though we are sinners, to exhibit that righteousness, and wisdom in our lives. We should have some control over that tongue James speaks about.

References

Stevenson, L. F. (1987). Seven theories of human nature. New York, New York: Oxford University Press.

A Study Of James - Part 4

"From whence come wars and fightings among you? come they not hence, even of your lusts that war in your members? Ye lust, and have not: ye kill, and desire to have, and cannot obtain: ye fight and war, yet ye have not, because ye ask not. Ye ask, and receive not, because ye ask amiss, that ye may consume it upon your lusts. Ye adulterers and adulteresses, know ye not that the friendship of the world is enmity with God? whosoever therefore will be a friend of the world is the enemy of God. Do ye think that the scripture saith in vain, The spirit that dwelleth in us lusteth to envy? But he giveth more grace. Wherefore he saith, God resisteth the proud, but giveth grace unto the humble. Submit yourselves therefore to God. Resist the devil, and he will flee from you. Draw nigh to God, and he will draw nigh to you. Cleanse your hands, ye sinners; and purify your hearts, ye double minded. Be afflicted, and mourn, and weep: let your laughter be turned to mourning, and your joy to heaviness. Humble yourselves in the sight of the Lord, and he shall lift you up" James 4:1-10 (KJV)

"From whence come wars and fightings among you? come they not hence, even of your lusts that war in your members?" Many years ago I showed an old roommate John these verses. He was preparing a paper and speech for a sociology class and needed some material that would reflect the despicable side of man concerning war. These verses sum up the cause of war simply and provide an excellent answer to why we have war. "Ye lust, and have not: ye kill, and desire to have, and cannot obtain: ye fight and war." Is there a more excellent way of reflecting upon and describing this reality of human nature? I think not. The above passages may be simple, but they strike to the heart of the issue of conflict and war.

War is a reality that can find absolutely no justification, only rationalization. There can be no justification for killing people for any reason. The law of God specifically qualifies this by saying "Thou shalt not kill" and we as people are expected to heed this law for it is very, very clear that God was and is not kidding concerning killing. However, we do rationalize this commandment especially concerning war. We fought World War I under the guise that we were out to make the world safe for democracy. We fought World War II under the idea that we were protecting ourselves. We were in Vietnam under the concept that we were protecting our interests. However, these rationalizations do not make war right and just. There might be a righteous war such as having taken on Hitler in World War II. However, that war wouldn't have had to be fought at all if it wasn't for the greed of power and oppression.

"Ye ask, and receive not, because ye ask amiss." The English Standard Version reads "You do not have; because you do not ask." The KJV indicates people don't have because they ask wrongly. The ESV asserts that people don't ask. I tend to think the ESV is probably wrong. That is to say, people may indeed ask but on failing to get what they want might use force to get it.

I think we can move now to a broader sense of not having what we desire than just thinking in terms of those things which cause War in the general sense of the word. I think now we can say we desire and do not have, so we take, or manipulate.

James blames our not having that which we desire because we do not ask in the right mind set. So, on a theological level we do ask. Often though as sinners, we ask from the wrong state of being, the state of being a sinner.

We cannot overlook though that we do fail to ask others for things, For example: I worked with an anesthesiologist who liked strawberry yogurt. However, every time she went through the dinner line at the hospital, they have other kinds of yogurt, but not strawberry. So she settled for something else. She never asked for strawberry yogurt. She'd come in and sit down with me and complain there wasn't any strawberry yogurt.

Now this is not a big issue but one which is bigger is seen in many of us. The problem is loneliness. No one comes to visit. However, are people invited to come? How about a dinner invitation? How about inviting people to Church and offer to give them a ride? Do we take the initiative here too? Or do we just hope people will just drop by?

Anyway, I have gotten off what James has written about here. Or have I, for he does not really specify who we are asking or what we are asking for. "Ye ask, and receive not, because ye ask amiss, that ye may consume it upon your lusts." Here James acknowledges that we ask wrongly, and oh how correct he is with this statement we ask wrongly "that ye may consume it upon your lusts." We do indeed tend to ask for things because of our own desires and covetousness. Can sinners be expected to perform in any other way? No, at least not until Sin is totally destroyed and eliminated with Christ's return. I do have some hope that with the help of the Holy Spirit, Christians can adopt a way of behaving that is in sync with what James is asserting here.

"Ye adulterers and adulteresses, know ye not that the friendship of the world is enmity with God?" As Christians we would have to say yes, for we cannot really become Christians until we recognize our friendship with the world and repent turning to God. We therefore would agree with James following statement: "whosoever therefore will be a friend of the world is the enemy of God." This is a strong statement. However, it means if we associate only with a world and not with God at all we alienate ourselves from God, it does not mean lack of appreciation for God's creation is needed to be on God's side. It means if we reject God as creator we have turned to worldly ideas and thus become God's enemy.

"Do ye think that the scripture saith in vain, The spirit that dwelleth in us lusteth to envy?" I admit I had trouble understanding what this verse was saying until I turned to other versions of scriptures and added some Pauline interpretation. This verse shows us why we acknowledge we have friendship with the world and hostility towards God and then why we turn to God. It is the Spirit yearning over us which helps us to realize this and then helps to accept more grace and helps us move in the following direction. However, remember we are still sinners and we will never reach these goals until Christ's presence or return. "God resisteth the proud, but giveth grace unto the humble."

"Submit yourselves therefore to God. Resist the devil, and he will flee from you. Draw nigh to God, and he will draw nigh to you. Cleanse your hands, ye sinners; and purify your hearts, ye double minded. Be afflicted, and mourn, and weep: let your laughter be turned to mourning, and your joy to heaviness. Humble yourselves in the sight of the Lord, and he shall lift you up." With instructions such as these, we have support for being responsible persons, not just spiritual puppets whose strings are pulled by God. Our choice though comes from being in a relationship with God. While sinners who are prone to resist God, God's presence influences our behavior.

"Speak not evil one of another, brethren. He that speaketh evil of his brother, and judgeth his brother, speaketh evil of the law, and judgeth the law: but if thou judge the law, thou art not a doer of the law, but a judge. There is one lawgiver, who is able to save and to destroy: who art thou that judgest another?" James 4:11-12 (KJV).

Once again, James reminds us of our relationship with the law and obeying it. Here he says we are not to speak evil against one another. By doing so, we speak evil against the law itself. James takes it even further and says we judge the law when we speak evil and are not doers of the law but judges. There is then a distinction. Doers are not judges. They live and practice the law. This does not put them in a position of being judgmental. To be judgmental is itself outside the domain of the law. So in essence we fall short of the glory of God in part by speaking evil. Since all of us have and will speak evil against our brothers and sisters, we have and will continue to fall short of the Glory of God in this way.

"There is one lawgiver, who is able to save and to destroy: who art thou that judgest another?" James now reminds us that God is the real judge and he alone can save us. Since we cannot even keep from speaking evil against our brothers and sisters, it is doubtful we are able to save ourselves. So we must recognize only God himself has the perfection we need to save us and we must turn to him for our salvation.

"Who art thou that judgest another?" James gives us a jab in the side. Just who do we think we are that we should speak evil against others? Are we so perfect we can take such liberties? Absolutely not! I think there are overtones of "Let him who is without sin cast the first stone" and "You see the speck in the eyes of other persons, you hypocrite remove the log from your own eye" before you pass judgment.

"Go to now, ye that say, Today or tomorrow we will go into such a city, and continue there a year, and buy and sell, and get gain: Whereas ye know not what shall be on the morrow. For what is your life? It is even a vapour, that appeareth for a little time, and then vanisheth away. For that ye ought to say, If the Lord will, we shall live, and do this, or that. But now ye rejoice in your boastings: all such rejoicing is evil. Therefore to him that knoweth to do good, and doeth it not, to him it is sin" James 4:13-17 (KJV).

"Today or tomorrow we will go into such a city, and continue there a year, and buy and sell, and get gain: Whereas ye know not what shall be on the morrow." All of us have made extravagant plans and really believed they would happen. Then we watched our dreams fade and be taken over with reality. My dream was to become the Great White Doctor. Then I changed it to the Great Psychiatrist. I went into nursing to get a head start on the others who were going to become doctors and also to help finance my way through pre-med studies. I never was good at studying though, but I kept hanging on to that dream. All through college I clung to it even though each year I knew my chances were slim to none to live out that dream. My grades kept getting better and my senior year I had a 3.8 average at Oglethorpe University. So I hung on to my expectations and hopes.

Fortunately, I had the sense to realize my calling may not be to medicine; but to the ministry. During the time I applied to medical school, I also applied to seminary, feeling God would take me where he wanted me to go. This is just one dream that changed. God had other plans for me. I know that is Calvinistic, but sometimes I really believe God does lead or at least some people down a path in life. James said, "If the Lord will, we shall live, and do this, or that."

James asks, "For what is your life? It is even a vapour, that appeareth for a little time, and then vanisheth away." I am continually amazed by how quickly the days go by now. The speed goes faster as I grow older. The comments of grown-ups to children "My, I can't get over how big you have grown" is now a reality to me. That is the way I talk to some young people on occasion, and the words of the song by Harry Belfonte, Alan Greene, & Malvina Reynolds song "Turn Around" include: "Turn around and you are tiny, turn around and you're grown, turn around and you're a young man going out of the door." The words from Shakespeare's Macbeth," Out, out brief candle, life's but a walking shadow, a poor player that struts and frets his hour upon the stage, and then is heard no more" speak to the quickness of life.

"But now ye rejoice in your boastings: all such rejoicing is evil." Yes, as it is we tend to pat ourselves on the back for the way things go in our lives. We say, "see, what I have done and how great I am." We do such boasting. How vain we can be? Our lives are full of gifts from God, not from ourselves.

"Therefore to him that knoweth to do good, and doeth it not, to him it is sin." I do not know where James got this idea. I cannot even be sure how it ties in with the instructions and comments he has been giving us except to say: OK, now you have heard the instructions. If you fail to do what is right, you deliberately sin and woe to the one who deliberately sins.

Lord, have mercy. Christ, have mercy. James has given us tough standards in faith, for faith

References

Belfonte, H., Greene, A., & Reynolds, M. (1957). *Turn Around*. Clara Music Publishing Corporation. http://people.wku.edu/charles.smith/MALVINA/mr175.htm.

A Study Of James - Part 5

"Go to now, ye rich men, weep and howl for your miseries that shall come upon you. Your riches are corrupted, and your garments are motheaten. Your gold and silver is cankered; and the rust of them shall be a witness against you, and shall eat your flesh as it were fire. Ye have heaped treasure together for the last days. Behold, the hire of the labourers who have reaped down your fields, which is of you kept back by fraud, crieth: and the cries of them which have reaped are entered into the ears of the Lord of sabaoth. Ye have lived in pleasure on the earth, and been wanton; ye have nourished your hearts, as in a day of slaughter. Ye have condemned and killed the just; and he doth not resist you" James 5:1-6 (KJV).

"Go to now, ye rich men, weep and howl for your miseries that shall come upon you." We need not be afraid of this statement for there is nothing wrong with accumulating wealth. It is selfish and greedy accumulation that we are concerned about here. When we accumulate our wealth only for ourselves without concern about how we get it, there is a problem. When wealth becomes a severe and significant problem for us causing stress and anxiety, it is not being accumulated in faith.

James does indeed indicate the Lord God will handle us firmly. "Your riches are corrupted, and your garments are motheaten. Your gold and silver is cankered; and the rust of them shall be a witness against you, and shall eat your flesh as it were fire. Ye have heaped treasure together for the last days." The accumulation of wealth is absolutely worthless for us in regard to eternity. We cannot take it with us. Further, consumption with becoming rich or being rich does not reflect Jesus' words found in Matthew 6:19: "Lay not up for yourselves treasures upon earth, where moth and rust doth corrupt, and where thieves break through and steal: But lay up for yourselves treasures in heaven, where neither moth nor rust doth corrupt, and where thieves do not break through nor steal: For where your treasure is, there will your heart be also"

Matthew 6:19-21 (KJV).

"Behold, the hire of the labourers who have reaped down your fields, which is of you kept back by fraud, crieth: and the cries of them which have reaped are entered into the ears of the Lord of sabaoth." Those who have been oppressed by those who have selfish ambition, who accumulated their wealth at the expense of other people, will be found with special rewards from God. For God has heard the cries of being misused and has heeded them. God has prepared special things for his people who are oppressed. They will be rewarded for their hard labors.

"Be patient therefore, brethren, unto the coming of the Lord. Behold, the husbandman waiteth for the precious fruit of the earth, and hath long patience for it, until he receive the early and latter rain. Be ye also patient; stablish your hearts: for the coming of the Lord draweth nigh. Grudge not one against another, brethren, lest ye be condemned: behold, the judge standeth before the door. Take, my brethren, the prophets, who have spoken in the name of the Lord, for an example of suffering affliction, and of patience. Behold, we count them happy which endure. Ye have heard of the patience of Job, and have seen the end of the Lord; that the Lord is very pitiful, and of tender mercy" James 5:7-11 (KJV).

"Be patient therefore, brethren, unto the coming of the Lord . . . stablish your hearts: for the coming of the Lord draweth nigh." It must be clearly understood that James believed here that the Christ was returning promptly. His advice for patience and establishing the heart are given under those expectations. One living today, however, finds it extremely hard to be patient during this age because for two thousand years Christians have been hearing that Christ is going to return soon. So we wait. We tend not to wait patiently because too many before us waited and died. So, there is often a lack of assurance that we will see the Christ before we die. We wait anxiously and not patiently.

"Grudge not one against another, brethren, lest ye be condemned: behold, the judge standeth before the door." All of our lives we have heard these instructions and have tried to follow them. However, it has to be noted we do not follow these instructions at many times in our life. We do tend to grumble and complain about many things. The great psychologist Abraham Maslow said that when one's life situation is improved, one does not eliminate the grumbling and complaining. Instead, a person raises the level of those things which are grumbled and complained about. So we see grumbling is a part of our lives and we would have to expect if we are still sinners, such grumbling will continue to take place.

"Behold, we count them happy which endure. Ye have heard of the patience of Job, and have seen the end of the Lord; that the Lord is very pitiful, and of tender mercy." You will recall that James starts off this letter by saying: "My brethren, count it all joy when ye fall into divers temptations; Knowing this, that the trying of your faith worketh patience." This indicates that by holding onto faith in God a person moves in the direction of completeness and wholeness. It means to keep on trusting God when things are not going right and when things are not working out the way they ought to be working out. This steadfastness leads to a happiness and joy. The Lord will provide the means for things to come as they ought to come about. It needs to be understood that, for those who hold steadfastly to their faith, God has much compassion and mercy. This compassion and mercy exists also for those who are not steadfast, but by not holding onto faith, a person rejects God's compassion and mercy. It is not God who is withholding His compassion and mercy. It is we who refuse to be steadfast in our hope and our faith who reject God's compassion and mercy.

"Is any among you afflicted? let him pray. Is any merry? let him sing psalms. Is any sick among you? let him call for the elders of the church; and let them pray over him, anointing him with oil in the name of the Lord: And the prayer of faith shall save the sick, and the Lord shall raise him up; and if he have committed sins, they shall be forgiven him. Confess your faults one to another, and pray one for another, that ye may be healed. The effectual fervent prayer of a righteous man availeth much. Elias was a man subject to like passions as we are, and he prayed earnestly that it might not rain: and it rained not on the earth by the space of three years and six months. And he prayed again, and the heaven gave rain, and the earth brought forth her fruit" James 5:13-18 (KJV).

"Is any among you afflicted? let him pray." It goes without saying that there is much suffering in the world. Let's think in terms of our own personal suffering here. These instructions are not meant for us to pray for the suffering of the world. They are meant for suffering which is within ourselves. Since all of us have suffering in our lives at some time, we can certainly afford to follow this advice: Pray.

Prayer needs to be offered to God during our time of suffering. If it doesn't bring healing, it is still a direct communication with God. That open channel of communication is a kind of healing. Prayer is the time we consciously and deliberately set aside to lift our problems and concerns to

God. It is healing in the sense that without the resource of prayer we have nothing to fall upon when a disease remains or threatens life. He encourages us to use prayer when we suffer.

"Is any merry? let him sing psalms." On the other side of life is joy. So we are instructed to express this joy through the singing of praise. Through praise we communicate our joy and happiness and excitement. It might be considered easy to sing praise when things are cheerful. Yet, in successful times, it is incredibly easy to forget to praise God. So James lets us know we are to express gratitude in our cheerfulness.

"Is any sick among you? let him call for the elders of the church; and let them pray over him, anointing him with oil in the name of the Lord." These instructions also are of great benefit to us when we are sick. We have a resource of comfort in calling on the elders of the Church to let them pray over us.

Now, I do not know if this means the elders have to come to our bedside or not, but in order to anoint us with oil, which we no longer do in this passage, they have to be at our bedside. So this is a very strong indication that the praying and the anointing is to take place beside us.

"And the prayer of faith shall save the sick . . . ." Notice this does not say "heal" the sick person in this translation. It says "save" the sick person. We should be careful in interpreting that the sick man will be healed right then and there for too many of us have seen the sick were not usually healed following prayer. Rather, we need to think in terms of a resurrection from the dead with Christ's return. With this resurrection, will be the healing for which was prayed. However, it needs to be understood the words of this verse "and the Lord shall raise him up" could very well mean instant healing. We cannot be closed to that possibility.

"And if he have committed sins, they shall be forgiven him." I sure hope this isn't limited to the sick. Since all have sinned and fall short of the glory of God, then it is quite obvious that we who are ill have sinned also. James is saying that, with the prayer of the elders, the sins which we have committed will be forgiven.

"Confess your faults one to another, and pray one for another, that ye may be healed." As sinners we are all instructed to confess our sins to each other. Now this does not mean you have to walk up before the whole of the congregation and confess your sins. I consider that to be a mistake. I am sure sinners, even as believers often fail to be very understanding or forgiving. Thus, one needs to make careful choices regarding confession. If you have a burden of sin in your heart, you had better tell someone who has enough faith to handle it.

Also we need to pray for each other so that we may be healed. Healing does not just come from our own prayers of faith. It comes in relationship to the prayers of faith of others.

"The effectual fervent prayer of a righteous man availeth much." Yes, this I firmly believe. A man who has faith in God and walks down the road of the Lord's way and obeys His commandments can pray great effective prayers. Unfortunately, only rarely in history has there ever been such a man. Elijah was one. Moses is another, and Jacob, and Isaiah, and of course most of all Jesus.

"Brethren, if any of you do err from the truth, and one convert him; Let him know, that he which converteth the sinner from the error of his way shall save a soul from death, and shall hide a multitude of sins" James 5:19-20 (KJV).

If one of us wanders from the truth, we will be as the sheep who has wandered from the flock. Thus, we will be subject to more harm for we will be at the mercy of the wolves. It is a very dangerous place to be and it could very well be for eternity. However, thanks be to God there is someone to bring us back to the truth. It is the Christ who has come to save us and redeem us. We must not think for a moment that we as sheep have the capabilities to bring back the lost to the truth. The only one who has these capabilities is Jesus Christ. Only he can bring: us back and only he can deliver us from the error of our way and save our souls from death and cover a multitude of sins. To think that a person, one of us, can do these things is a misinterpretation of these verses. Verses 19 - 20 describe only what the Christ can do and remind us not to forget that.

Printed in the United States
By Bookmasters